The Community
of Cinema

The Community
of Cinema
How Cinema and Spectacle
Transformed the American Downtown

JAMES FORSHER

Westport, Connecticut
London

Library of Congress Cataloging-in-Publication Data

Forsher, James, 1953–
    The community of cinema : how cinema and spectacle transformed the
American downtown / James Forsher.
        p.   cm.
    Includes bibliographical references and index.
    ISBN 0–275–97355–7 (alk. paper)
    1. Motion pictures—Social aspects—United States.   2. Motion picture
theaters—United States—History.   3. United States—Social life and
customs—20th century.   I. Title.
PN1995.9.S6 F67   2003
302.23′43′0973—dc21   2002028762

British Library Cataloguing in Publication Data is available.

Library of Congress Catalog Card Number: 2002028762
ISBN: 0–275–97355–7

First published in 2003

Praeger Publishers, 88 Post Road West, Westport, CT 06881
An imprint of Greenwood Publishing Group, Inc.
www.praeger.com

Printed in the United States of America

The paper used in this book complies with the
Permanent Paper Standard issued by the National
Information Standards Organization (Z39.48–1984).

10 9 8 7 6 5 4 3 2 1

Copyright Acknowledgments

The author and publisher gratefully acknowledge permission for use of the
following material:

Excerpts from Allen Michaan's December 2001 interview as well as photos of
the Grand Lake Theatre.

Excerpts from Hamid Hashemi's October 2001 interview as well as photos of
Muvico Theaters.

Contents

Preface

Nearly every town in America has had one. Its architectural frontage has become an icon of Main Street itself. With the tremendous volume of movie theaters that cover the United States, the questions arise: What effect did theaters have on the social life of towns? How did small movie theaters and larger movie palaces affect the physical design of downtown America during the past century? How did the theater affect the vitality of downtown America? While motion-picture exhibition may not be typical topics of urban-studies literature, these questions are at the heart of this book.

In addition to exploring the points just noted, this book attempts to bridge the various fields that are affected by cinema's impact on culture and form. The movie theater has created its own community, which will be referred to in this book as "the community of the cinema," with its own architectural styles, its own neighborhood districts, its own cultural rules of behavior and its own language.

In addition to focusing on the community of cinema, this book looks at how the movie theater has created a unique sense of place. Each chapter examines how the community of cinema evolved over its century-long history and the changes it instituted in the downtown and neighborhood shopping districts it has populated, as well as its contribution to the sense of community it added to our society.

This book was inspired by my lifelong love affair with the movie theater. When I was a toddler, my weekends were often highlighted by visits to the nearby Olympic Drive-in located a few miles away in Los Angeles, California. My family would pile into a car and go to the drive-in an hour before the film began, allowing me the ritual of somewhat awkwardly going to the playground in my pajamas, going to the snack bar, watching the cartoons and waking up the next morning somehow magically transported into my bed at home.

During my elementary and junior-high-school years, I went weekly with friends to the Pickwood Theatre down the street on Pico Boulevard, again creating a ritual of a film and a snack at the local hamburger stand immediately afterwards. In high school, drive-ins and my first car, a Volkswagen Camper, were parts of a multitude of stories that do not belong on these pages. In short, I cannot separate my leisure time growing up and the cinema.

On a recent trip around the country, my family and I, in a very unscientific but time-consuming activity, went looking for theaters in the multitude of small towns and cities that we passed through. Wherever we went, we discovered a relationship between the health of a street and the condition of the movie houses on the block. What I observed supported the theme of this book: Healthy blocks often had a vibrant movie theater in nearby proximity. Dying blocks had no theaters or recently closed ones. As the following pages will examine, the movie theater and healthy urban districts have a strong and historic link.

I would like to thank Dr. Tridib Banerjee, Dr. William Dutton and Dr. William Baer of the University of Southern California for help in developing my initial research. I also want to thank Dr. Steve McDowell and Dr. Barney Warf, my colleagues at Florida State University for their input during the writing stage of the manuscript. Special thanks also go to Allen Michaan of Renaissance Rialto Theaters and Hamid Hashemi of Muvico Theaters, who were both extremely helpful in contributing their time and effort in explaining the contemporary state of exhibition. Richard Sklenar, executive director of the Theatre Historical Society of America, was invaluable in his advice and research materials. Thanks also to Dr. James N. Eaton, Florida A&M University's Black Archives and Tallahassee historian Anne Roberts.

Finally, I want to thank my wife Neena and daughter Lily for their kindness and understanding during the hours I was hidden away writing this book in our home office.

Introduction

How has the movie theater affected the communities it has moved into? From its earliest days, the movie theater and entertainment district became a decidedly fixed location that affected transportation patterns and created a style of social interaction that permeated the entire century. The movie theater became a social institution, attracting its own clientele and serving as a draw for local retail establishments. It fostered civility and a chance for neighbors to stay in touch, challenging more traditional places to congregate, such as churches, bars, work arenas and restaurants.

The movie theater became a destination that served as an anchor for surrounding businesses. It attracted people from various neighborhoods to a shared location. "The community of cinema" also created social relationships through the power of its messages and images, uniting millions in love affairs with actresses, anger toward gangsters or awe of a ship sinking. The community of cinema has become an American institution.

WHAT MAKES A COMMUNITY?

The attempt to define community and public space has historically been linked to such terms as "public sector" and "public realm." To Rousseau (1968), the public realm was defined by how well citizens

Fotosho Theatre. Miami, Florida. June, 1921. (Photo courtesy of the Florida State Archives)

participated in the affairs of government; the better constituted the state, the more public affairs outweighed private ones in the minds of its citizens. Tocqueville (1971) referred to a "political society," and Habermas (1974) described community as the "public sphere." Arendt (1979) has described the "public realm" as a distinctive field of action that can emerge whenever human beings act and deliberate in concert.

Contemporary society, heavily saturated with images and iconography, has in fact redefined its own meaning of communities based on "place." New definitions of place and community have expanded its meaning, including the environment by which people shape the physical attributes of the city by the destinations they can reach—cities based more on the transportation paths and the time they take as opposed to the physical space alone. Langdon Winner (1992) suggested that the time has come to discard our "place-oriented theories" because they have become obsolete.

A CONSUMER CULTURE

The turn of the twentieth century witnessed the development of a culture that can be described by its consumption and leisure activities. This early consumer culture has had an important and lasting impact on how we define culture today. The rise of a consumer culture represented a new mechanism of controlling and influencing the population. Old traditions broke down as the nation became increasingly more diversified and consumerism promoted social reconciliation (Cotkin 1992). Americans from all classes, races and economic backgrounds shared in the desire for consumer merchandise.

With the culture of consumption and leisure came new symbols to define the modern age. Consumption was guided by societal standards resulting from similar people making similar choices. With the rise of the department store and modern forms of entertainment, a culture based on the possibility of defining oneself through desire and enjoyment seemed closer at hand. By the turn of the twentieth century, consumerism helped to define modern American culture (Cotkin 1992). What "institution" serves better as a mirror of the consumption patterns and growing leisure choices than the movie theater?

THE POWER OF CINEMA

From the earliest days of film production, writers and producers faced the challenge of writing stories that would speak to all Americans. They realized the challenge they faced as filmmakers was to find stories that would speak to everyone, that would create a "common meaning" for the divergent masses that comprised the United States at the turn of the century.

One of the greatest problems in doing so were the prejudices the actual filmmakers and studio bosses themselves held. D.W. Griffith, considered to be one of the greatest storytellers in cinema history, ran into problems when his deeply routed southern views became predominantly displayed within the storyline of his 1915 production, *The Birth of a Nation*. From coast to coast the film was boycotted and banned due to its explicit racist caricatures of African Americans, yet Griffith remained angered and shocked at this reaction. In a reply to a critical editorial the *New York Globe* wrote about his film, Griffith explained his dismay at the negative comments about his portrayal of African Americans in the film, pointing out, "We show many phases of the question and we do pay particular attention to those faithful Negroes who stayed with their former masters and were ready to give up their lives to protect their white friends. No characters in the story are applauded with greater fervor than the good Negroes whose devotion is so clearly shown" (Griffith 1915).

Despite the problems exemplified by such films as *The Birth of a Nation*, cinema was for the most part successful in finding a common voice that was acceptable to most audiences. The motion-picture theater became the mouthpiece for the greatest mass-communication technology man had ever invented.

Motion pictures forced a dialogue throughout America that exposed a wide rift in values and definitions of obscenity and of decency. The motion-picture industry had to find a way to create films that could be played to divergent communities. In that quest, it helped create a modern definition of community.

The movie theater and our contemporary definition of public space have a strong relationship. The theater created an atmosphere for public gatherings, both in the theater and out on the streets bordering the entertainment district. Even if the cinema was privately owned, it adhered to a somewhat democratic openness in its audience makeup. The community at large gathered and experienced a public space that represented a place that allowed various neighborhoods, work places and cultures to interact. The common denominator was the civility of the gathering and the shared message that the films projected.

The introduction of the motion-picture theater had a multifold impact on the urban environment. With the proliferation of motion-picture theaters, entertainment districts formed, and by the early 1900s, a symbiotic relationship with commercial districts developed that spanned the entire twentieth century, evolving to today's manifestation of retail environment and entertainment: the mall.

In contemporary society, movie theaters and the malls that hold many of them have evolved in their sense of defining community. Commercial malls have become an alternative to the traditional Main Street, and in fact, may be considered the new Main Streets of the the twenty-first century. Retail locations such as the Mall of America in Minnesota or the West Edmonton Mall in Canada have taken on a theme-park atmosphere. They are also, in Michael Sorkin's words, contributing to the "Disneyitis" of America in which the city is a simulation of television, a theme park in which architecture is preoccupied with reproducing urban disguises (1992, p.xiii). Edward

Soja describes the new urban environment as one in which everything is possible and nothing is real (1992, p.121).

Trying to apply contemporary definitions of "place" to past community structures is a tricky business. However, the differences between today's modern mall and the Main Street of 1920 may not be all that great. Contemporary descriptions of spectacle environments in malls and retail environments could also be used to describe the earlier spectacle environment created by the palace cinemas from the turn of the century through the Depression.

MOVIE THEATERS AS INDICATORS OF URBAN VITALITY

The growth and decay of the central business district cannot be examined without including the influence of the entertainment district on the development, demise and rebirth of downtown America. The following chapters explore the significance of the entertainment district, the effects its demise has had on the urban core and the impact of its reemergence into contemporary culture.

The relationship between films, shopping and social interaction today may seem very contemporary, but it is one that literally goes back to the first days of the movies. The discussion of the relationship between the entertainment district and retail environments in the central business district as well as neighborhood retail districts is imperative in understanding the changes in commerce, transportation, retail business, neighborhoods and all other elements of urban life during the twentieth century.

One can argue that the entertainment district, in a deterministic manner, has followed the development of communities throughout America. I argue the opposite—that the entertainment district itself may in fact have created its own sense of community, one with its own architectural style, rules of social engagement, geographies and rules of economy.

As the community of cinema grew in importance, it began to have its own ripple effects on surrounding businesses as it changed locations and audiences over the years. When movie palaces started closing in large numbers during the early 1930s, the loss of tens of thousands of attendees also affected the greater downtown business and retail core that they had helped nurture and develop.

The community of cinema also became a victim of societal changes in suburban living, transportation and new technologies. It should be no surprise that one of the most difficult periods for motion-picture production and exhibition coincided with both the introduction of television and a noticeable deterioration in central business district retail activities.

The concept of an entertainment district poses a series of conflicting theoretical implications. Several questions are central to the relationship between the entertainment district and the development and growth of urban vitality. Did the entertainment district help create and define the central business district in large American cities? Did it then contribute to the central business district's demise by its departure?

The entertainment district developed during the same period in which the suburban neighborhoods developed in America. Entertainment districts were located both in the downtown and in neighborhood retail districts. What was the relationship between entertainment districts' eventual abandonment of the downtown, the move to the suburbs and the development of suburban growth and the branching out of retail establishments?

The entertainment district created the largest gathering space for diverse groups of Americans. It represented in many ways the democratic socialization of American society during the early part of the twentieth century. Never before had groups from so many economic and racial backgrounds gathered and shared a common experience on a weekly basis. However, African Americans were largely banned from the movie theaters during the first six decades of the theater's existence. How did the entertainment district on one hand foster greater understanding among different ethnic groups in America, yet uphold segregationist policies against African Americans?

This book examines the preceding questions in both a cultural and historical context. The story of the entertainment district's hundred-year relationship with the city is told by investigating both its physical evolution and its effect on American culture histories that never existed. Within this story, while not directly addressed, is the century-long history of the thousands of films that attracted the audiences and contributed to the common dreams and fantasies that they supplied. With the combination of films and theaters, America's cities and towns have become, for all practical purposes, a community of cinema.

Part One

From Storefront to Palace

Chapter 1

The Community of Cinema

Among the multitude of inventions Thomas Edison's laboratories worked on in the early 1890s, one area of research included experimenting with motion pictures. An Edison research scientist, W.K.L. Dickson, perfected the kinetoscope, a machine that could play a short film in a large viewing box. Edison took the opportunity of demonstrating the device at the Chicago World's Fair of 1893. Among those attending was a middle-aged furrier named Adolph Zukor who would later recall seeing the film, one he remembered being about 30 seconds in length. "From that day on," he reminisced, "I had motion pictures on my mind" (interview with Adolph Zukor, 1967).

Edison soon began to license his kinetoscope to penny-arcade proprietors, with the first kinetoscope parlor opening in New York on April 6, 1894. The penny-arcade parlor was located close to the Union Square commercial and retail shopping districts in New York and attracted interest immediately. Soon the city had several of these penny-arcade entertainment parlors, attracting huge crowds who were instantly amazed at the new technology that allowed them to see moving images of far-off cities, famous Americans and unusual events. As crowds grew, more and more entrepreneurs opened up penny arcades not only in New York but all across America.

Over the next several years, Adolph Zukor kept an eye on the growing technology and finally was offered an investment opportu-

Matanzas Theatre, St. Augustine, Florida, 1951. *Distant Drums*, an action drama starring Gary Cooper and set in Florida during the Seminole Indian uprising, had a local premiere at the Matanzas. The event featured the Hewt Perry Aquatic Theatre and attracted hundreds of participants to the city's commercial district. (Photo courtesy of the Florida State Archives)

nity in the penny-arcade business in the early 1900s. He bought into an arcade on 14th Street near 7th Avenue. Zukor soon realized that he wanted to get out of the fur trade; during the entertainment parlor's first year of operation, the arcade generated $100,000 in pennies. This partnership soon fell apart, and Zukor was bought out. Zukor, however, went looking for other opportunities and found one in an unusual arcade attraction called Hale's Tours.

George Hale was the fire chief in Kansas City, Missouri, at the turn of the last century. He was also an inventor and entrepreneur with an interest in the new technologies of motion-picture projection. He had the opportunity of traveling to London's Crystal Palace for a show demonstrating fire-fighting equipment at which he won top prizes for his work. While he was there, he began to study the spectacular environment that the show was in as well as the manner of presentation that entertained hundreds of people. Hale became inspired by what he saw and came up with the idea of combining travel locations and motion pictures. He decided that for films to succeed, one needed to add a sense of spectacle to motion picture exhibition. When he returned to the United States, he developed and demonstrated a theater concept called "Hale's Tours and Scenes of the World" at the St. Louis World's Fair of 1903. He had created a motion-picture theater that mimicked a railroad-car environment; this

Hale's Tours, Adolph Zukor's first motion picture theater. (Author's collection)

at a time when no dedicated motion-picture houses were successfully operating. It met with great interest, and Hale began to syndicate his show. The New York licensee was Adolph Zukor.

"Hale's Tours" was not a penny arcade. Instead, it used motion-picture projection technology that had been around for nearly five years but had been greatly underutilized. Hale's movie theater was different from any other, decorated to look like the interior of a railroad car. The film theater as a spectacle had been introduced into America's largest central business district.

Zukor found a location for his Hale's Tours at 46 Union Square South, next to an existing penny arcade. Zukor saw an important connection between street traffic, retail areas and his business. From his experience owning a penny arcade, he projected that a large volume of people willing to spend a penny for a unique experience would make his venture profitable (Irwin 1928, p.100).

Zukor built a train-entrance platform and opened the theater for exhibition. Within the first week, he had a line half a block long waiting at all times for admission. After the first week, the attendance began to decline. Zukor soon realized that the gimmick of a railroad-car theater alone would not sustain an audience. He discovered that an exhibitor also needed to offer a variety of entertaining films. At about the same time, he saw a screening of the movie *The Great Train Robbery* and was captivated by its story line, reinforcing his opinion that entertainment on the screen was just as important as the environment of the theater. He soon began changing the film titles every few days, and attendance once again rose. Zukor learned some important lessons from this experience, lessons that eventually led him to a career as the chairman of the board of Paramount Studios as well as the Paramount Theater chain. Other penny-arcade owners at the time who were having similar experiences included men like MGM's Marcus Loew, the Warner brothers, and Universal's Carl Laemmle.

From this simplest of theater designs came the inspiration for the American movie theater. Spectacle and entertainment would soon give shape to redefining the look and structure of retail districts across America and help develop America's amusement culture for the next 100 years.

Chapter 2

It Started with a Nickel

Thomas Edison spent a decade perfecting motion-picture production. By all rights, he should have been able to claim to be the founder of the first motion-picture theater. At worst, he should have supplied the technology for it. After all, the history of the community of cinema can be traced back to the turn of the twentieth century when the first motion pictures in the United States were developed and marketed by Thomas Edison. Edison set up a distribution business that licensed his projectors and films to local entrepreneurs throughout the country. But none of this led directly to the first dedicated and successful movie theater.

Edison believed in the future of motion pictures and envisioned that they would indeed be a popular attraction. His patented devices were springing up in penny arcades around the country, showing brief films through a peephole in his kinetoscope. In April 1896, Edison's company even sponsored and showed a half hour of "projected films" using the vitascope as part of a vaudeville show. A motion picture and a vaudeville performance soon became a common combination, with few exhibitors interested in showing films by themselves. Edison's intense scrutiny in keeping his patents did not allow users to deviate from what Edison's Motion Picture Patents Company would approve. Dedicated feature-film use was not part of the plan.

Pittsburgh, Pennsylvania, 1905. The Nickelodeon was the first successful dedicated movie theater in America, and helped begin the nickel theater craze that swept the country. (Photo courtesy of Carnegie Library of Pittsburgh)

Thousands of penny arcades and vaudeville theaters were showing films around the entire country. One would think that the idea for a dedicated movie house would have developed in the early entertainment districts composed of penny arcades. However, the first successful movie house began in—of all places—Pittsburgh, Pennsylvania.

The year was 1905, and two enterprising exhibitors named Harry Davis and John P. Harris had a vision. The short films that entertained audiences between vaudeville acts and in the machines located at penny arcades might, they guessed, bring in audiences on their own. This was not a novel concept, and exhibitors could nervously point to the failure of Tally's theater in downtown Los Angeles just three years before. In 1902, Los Angeles became the site for the first theater dedicated to films, the Electric Theater, located at 262 Main Street. The theater advertised itself as featuring "up-to-date high-class moving picture entertainment, especially for ladies and children," and charged 10 cents for admission (Ramsaye 1926, p.425). It soon failed when Tally closed his operation after a few months and left town.

However, Harris and Davis believed in their vision and would not be deterred. Perhaps audiences were more familiar with films, or the quality of the films themselves had improved. Whatever the case, their gut-level feeling could not have been more correct, and they were willing to bet $40,000 on the experiment ("The Nickelodeon" 1907, p.140). On June 5, 1905, they opened to sellout crowds who showed up at their "Nickelodeon," the name they had given their theater in honor of the admission price.

Within months, Davis and Harris saw that their success was not a product of mere novelty but had become a new principal form of entertainment for thousands of children and adults. From eight in the morning until midnight, the Nickelodeon theater stayed open. This storeroom converted into a theater had fewer than 100 seats, but over the course of a day, 7,000 spectators came through the doors. As *The Dispatcher*, a local Pittsburgh paper, described the Nickelodeon, "It was in the broadest sense of the phrase a theater for the people" (Lightner 1919).

The Nickelodeon's success helped create the second dedicated movie theater. This one opened not in the United States, but in Warsaw, Poland, when a Pittsburgh resident of Polish origin observed the successes of the Pittsburgh Nickelodeon and recognized the possibilities of opening a theater in his native country. The nickelodeon craze had begun.

Harris and Davis soon expanded the size of their operation by opening the much larger Lyric Theatre. They then proceeded to open 18 more store-theaters around town and were joined by dozens of other exhibitors who watched their success and wanted some share in it. The urban landscape of downtown Pittsburgh and its various neighborhoods were changed to reflect the ubiquitous theater marquees that announced the latest films being shown.

To get around Edison's patents, Harris and Davis purchased the first projection device manufactured in the world, the Lumière brothers' cinematograph. Films were available from independent American producers as well as foreign distributors, allowing for the bypassing of Edison's film-distribution arm. It did not take long for Edison to realize that his company would have to change its idea of film exhibition if it was to survive.

America literally went movie crazy. By May 1907, *Moving Picture World*, a newly created weekly magazine dedicated to the growing film-production and exhibition business, had estimated that between 2,500 and 3,000 "5-cent theaters" had opened around the country ("The Nickelodeon" 1907, p.140). The "nickel place of amusement," as some called it, was a relatively simple operation. Typically a carnival barker sat on the street, exclaiming that "for only a nickel, five pennies, a half of a dime" one could see a show that would last 15 minutes. The theater was a simple concept in both its design and function. *Moving Picture World* itemized in a few sentences all the ingredients a person would need to open his own 5-cent theater:

> One storeroom, seating from 200 to 500 persons
> One phonograph with extra large horn
> One young woman cashier
> One electric sign
> One cinematograph, with operator
> One canvas on which to throw the pictures
> One piano
> One barker
> One manager
> As many chairs as the store will hold
> A few brains and a little tact. Mix pepper and salt to taste.
> ("The Nickelodeon" 1907, p.140)

In the earliest years, the majority of 5-cent theater owners received their films from abroad, avoiding the patent claims of Edison's patent outfit. Exhibitors bought films by the foot from production centers in Paris and London. Because exhibitors owned the film, sections of film that film operators found boring could be simply cut out by a snip of the scissors.

Theater owners understood that to attract an audience, an affordable admission was necessary. What they also provided was an affordable, accessible and socially approved community gathering space. Every city and town across America adopted the movie theater. An estimated 96 million Americans were living in the United States in 1914 (U.S. Bureau of the Census), and an estimated 26 million went weekly to the theater.[1] This was the beginning of what Nasaw (1993) refers to as the "amusement culture" of movies.

The effects on culture and the development of community may be debatable in the philosophical sense, but the effects on society were profound. One of the greatest influences on contemporary urban culture, motion pictures literally began to change society as soon as the technology was introduced at the turn of the century. *Moving Picture World* in May 1907 noted that the 5-cent theater was beginning to play an important part in the functioning of city life. "They have been looked upon largely as places of trivial amusement, not calling for any serious consideration. They seem, however, to be something that may become one of the greatest forces for good or for evil in the city" ("The Nickelodeon" 1907, p.140). *Moving Picture World* went on to point out how the theater had already proven itself to be a force for helping families and supplying entertainment in the crowded inner city. "In the congested districts the 5-cent theaters are proving a source of much innocent entertainment. The mothers do not have to dress to attend them, and they take the children and spend many restful hours in them at very small expense" ("The Nickelodeon" 1907, p.140).

In a matter of months, the city was changing, and the changes were occurring to such a noticeable degree that they became a subject of national debate. Some writers called for the end of the nickelodeon, charging that the theaters were dangerous to both public morality and health. The second charge had some substance when it became public knowledge that "certain owners are in the habit of buying old and worn-out machines of types that existed in the early days of cinematography, and by tinkering them, adding a little here and little there, making them work (in a fashion). The result has been disastrous fires caused through this inefficiency and carelessness" (*Moving Picture World* March 16, 1907, p.20). The city of New York went so far as to close all nickelodeons in early 1907 due to fears of fire and dangers to health ("The Closing" 1907, p.20). This was an era of change in which few dared project what the future of the movie theater could be.

NOTE

1. Sources such as *Moving Picture World* and exhibition companies attempted to come up with weekly attendance figures, but they are difficult to ascertain due to the volume of theaters, exhibitors and locations. Nevertheless, the blossoming number of theaters speaks to an immense public turnout.

Chapter 3

Entertainment Districts and the New American Downtown

Why did the nickelodeon become such a success so quickly? Part of the answer may simply lie in the timing. By the turn of the twentieth century, members of the expanding working class began to find themselves with less time at work and more money for leisure activities, but few precedents on how to fill their leisure time. Cities during the latter part of the nineteenth century may have had amusement activities, but the central business districts were limited in free-time activities by a combination of factors. Playhouses largely appealed to the upper-income class. Saloons were largely the domain of adult males. Weather limited parades. Amusement parks became the predominant form of mass-culture amusement, but they were often physically located away from the primary urban core. For the growing number of middle-class citizens of the city, few options were available (Nasaw 1993, p.15).

Transportation had also become more accessible for those working in the inner city. At the beginning of the 1890s, only 15 percent of streetcars were electrified. By 1902, however, more than 94 percent of streetcars had been converted from horse-drawn streetcars to electrically operated equipment. Since the fare was typically a nickel, the city became available to a growing number of citizens, and office workers had the option of living outside the immediate downtown. Shoppers used the streetcars to live in residential neighborhoods and

work in the central business district, influencing the creation of retail and entertainment districts in the urban core as well as surrounding suburban neighborhoods. With more disposable income, free time
and greater access to the central business districts for all urban Americans, the city was becoming a place both to work and to play.

THE PENNY ARCADE AND THE MOVIE THEATER

As early as the 1890s, limited entertainment districts began to
develop in major American cities, featuring vaudeville theaters, playhouses and penny arcades, which were introduced in 1894. These
areas, located strategically close to both white-collar employees and
"ladies' shopping districts" (Rifkind 1977) were often defined by the
mix of theaters and retail establishments. These districts developed
across the country, taking on the identification of a major street like
New York's Broadway or the one theater in the middle of a small
midwestern or New England town's main street.

Savoy Theatre, Jacksonville, Florida, corner of Main and Forsyth. The
Savoy had become the center of a vibrant commercial district. (Courtesy
of the Florida State Archives)

While live theater and vaudeville flourished, the novelty of the penny arcade did not last, and within a year crowds began to dwindle. Parlor operators did not find wide crowds again until the Spanish-American War in 1898, when interest in actual moving pictures of the war attracted audiences. At the war's end, the parlors once again began to lose business.

Penny-arcade owners discovered that they had to create environments that attracted customers. The penny arcade had to locate in areas with heavy street traffic and offer programs that the public wanted to see. Many arcades went head-to-head with vaudeville theaters and also offered moving-picture exhibitions in back rooms or upstairs. At best, it was a volatile time.

As the popularity of the vaudeville and penny arcades with projected movies grew, the number of facilities featuring these shows increased. The majority of institutions continued to open up establishments in and around the central business district. They found their customers to be largely composed of the white-collar workforce and their families. They also found that being in or near retail districts contributed to an audience base, a match of amusement and retail outlets that continues to the present day.

Whether watched through the peephole in an arcade's motion-picture machine or projected on a screen, the earliest films were typically "actualities," short motion pictures of actual events that were taking place literally around the world. The dramatic film was introduced in 1903 when filmmaker Edwin S. Porter made *The Great Train Robbery*, which featured an action-packed story of bandits and lawmen. At the same time in France, filmmaker Georges Méliès produced moving pictures that brought fantasies to the screen, with stories that included dancing devils, a trip to the moon and voyages to the bottom of the sea.

When the 5-cent theater entered the picture in late 1905, the concept of motion-picture entertainment shifted from a by-product of a vaudeville show or arcade offering to an entertainment medium on its own. The nickelodeon at its outset often occupied little more than a storefront. As crowds grew and larger spaces were needed, theater owners, most of whom came out of vaudeville, used vaudeville and live theaters as models for the space to project the film shows. Theaters could be as sparse as a room with curtains and chairs, or a live theater with ornamentation could be refurbished. However, film exhibitors began to compete with each other for audiences, and the amusement-park sideshow began to be transplanted to Main Street as theater managers tried everything possible to entice audiences into shows. Music, barkers and marquees began to promote a spectacle environment in the increasingly large theaters that began to replace storefront theater operations.

By 1908, storefronts gave way to legitimate houses with amenities that made going to the theater easier and more attractive. The ornamentation that began to mark vaudeville theaters in the late 1890s soon began to appear in motion-picture theaters. Advertisements were oriented to middle-class audiences, especially women, and theater entrances were opened up to let audiences see that no mischief was occurring inside. It was not unusual to find snack bars, candy stores and cafés near the theaters, offering beverages and food items aimed toward theater patrons, the precursors of the snack bars that would appear more than two decades later in theaters themselves.

The nickelodeons soon began to create separate and unusual identities. Many set their entrances back by at least six feet. Others created iconographic images in front of the theater. In Seattle, the Liberty Theatre created a 40-foot-tall "Statue of Liberty" that was surrounded by hundreds of lights. The novelty of this site reportedly caused street riots that required police crowd control (Hulfish 1918). Other theaters created "butterfly" motifs, Greek temples and Moorish temples.

The motion picture entertainment district quickly developed audiences comprised largely of men, children and older women representing both native-born persons and foreign immigrants (Stones 1993, pp.22–23). The only group at this time not attending the theaters in large numbers was single women 16 to 30 years of age. This may have been due to social pressure against going to an amusement activity without a chaperone, or it may have reflected the long work hours many women at this age had to endure.

The proliferation of theaters near popular retail districts soon had a profound effect on the city. The new entertainment districts began to create an environment for the central city that would forever help define the look, feel and usage of downtown America. By coming to the movies, thousands of residents each day created a sense of civic sociability that had not existed just five years before, allowing residents to gather for no other purpose than entertainment. Regardless of what part of the city they lived in, what church they attended or what job they held, they intermingled. The public spaces outside the theaters, on the roads to the districts or on the streets in front of the districts evolved to become a magical world that would soon be nick-named the "Great White Way" all across America.

In hindsight, the term "Great White Way" had a separate conno-tation. The masses that came to these theaters were a cross section of society, but which society? The theaters of America in the early 1900s began to reflect the greater social segregation that was affect-ing cities not only in the South, but also across the nation. The grow-ing sense of racism was manifested in the rules of admission in theaters, and black Americans faced exclusion not only in housing, work and education but even in the medium that held the greatest promise to include Americans of all economic and social classes: motion pictures.

The new and bawdy nature of the medium was not free of con-troversy and as motion pictures spread, they began to offend the more conservative members of communities throughout the United States. To many people, the early movie theaters attracted a problematic crowd and they feared that nickel theaters would cause blight to their communities.

The motion-picture theater was causing a major challenge to the order of the modern American city. What was happening was a change in how a community would shop, entertain itself and social-ize. It was the beginning of the urban form of the entertainment dis-trict that was developing in every town and city in America.

THE NEW YORK ENTERTAINMENT DISTRICT, 1880–1915

The movie theater's popularity was not limited to New York, but if any town can claim to have been a founding home to the commu-nity of cinema, it was here. The technologies for film may have de-veloped throughout the country, but there was no better place for demonstrating the possibilities of the new technologies' impact on a community than New York City.

As America's largest city, by 1910 New York had grown to a popu-lation of 4,766,883 (U.S. Bureau of the Census). The population was composed of a substantial number of citizens not born in the United States, with an estimated 1,944,357 in 1910, or 40 percent of the city's population. These immigrants were particularly important to the growth of the community of cinema. The community of cinema was one of the earliest environments that helped define what would eventually be described as a "mixing-bowl" society found at the turn of the century. It was a safe environment for newcomers to find out what was American in the comfort of their neighborhoods.

As early as 1880, New York had developed a thriving entertainment district that was centered on Broadway between Canal and Houston, within walking distance of many of the city's main retail establishments. A number of live stage theaters had opened earlier, such as the Olympic in 1837, and by the 1860s, several live stage theaters, as well as half a dozen minstrel halls, were located in this section of Broadway (Dunlap 1990). Even in these early years, the mix of entertainment and retail shopping became obvious to store owners, and the area became the home of such legendary New York retail establishments as Lord and Taylor in 1860, Brooks Brothers in 1858, and Tiffany's at 550 Broadway in 1864.

The district also had a number of concert saloons, which were largely drinking institutions that featured singing and dancing. High culture was also served by the likes of the Eden Musee, considered one of the best museums in the nation, and within walking distance from the "ladies' mile." But the clientele for museums and saloons was far different from those who attended the live stage theaters.

Live theater was popular, but because of its expense, it was not geared to the general population. During the 1870s and 1880s, the typical seat prices rose to an extravagant one-dollar. Upper-class theatergoers had no problem with these fees, but the majority of New Yorkers found themselves economically excluded.

By the turn of the century, a new form of theater began to appeal to the working population. The most popular of the variety theaters were the vaudeville establishments, like the Theatre Comique, which drew patrons by a promise of fun entertainment at a price all could afford. Among the patrons were a growing number of housewives who filled in their shopping day by attending amusement activities.

The modern theater, whether for live or motion-picture presentation, was designed from its earliest inception to be a fantasy environment. The physical design that visibly shaped the turn-of-the-century entertainment district was inspired by a combination of amusement parks and contemporary architectural revivals of classic styles such as Greek, Roman and beaux arts, as well as high-culture entertainment theaters that had previously been aimed at upper-income theatergoers.

The New York entertainment district began to move north by the late 1870s, as the retail district moved in search of larger and more modern facilities. The "ladies' mile" appeared near Union Square and

23rd Street. Arnold Constable and Company in 1859 was the first major retail institution to move into the area. Lord and Taylor followed in 1870. Before long, almost every major commercial business had a location in and around Union Square, including Bell Telephone (1872), Gorham Silver and W.J. Sloane, which moved to 880 Broadway in 1881.

America went vaudeville crazy between 1890 and 1900, with the number of touring vaudeville acts growing from 50 to 500 (Nasaw 1993, p.4). The vaudeville audience changed America's relationship with entertainment. Gone were the days of "restrained emotions" as Richard Sennett has referred to those of middle-class audiences (1977, p.206). The vaudeville audience was enticed to let it all out.

New York's vaudeville entertainment congregated on 14th Street and 23rd Street with institutions like the Proctor Theatre. New York was the perfect breeding ground for an entertainment district fostered by vaudeville theaters. An increasingly large working class accompanied by a growing leisure class guaranteed audiences to theaters close enough to the commercial zones. The shows promised "respectability" in their delivery and a safe haven for working women. They made the theater a community gathering place to which it was safe for all to come. The audiences were largely comprised of lower-class, white-collar workers, many of whom were women. Studies of working habits during this time showed that most of the recreation time and money was spent either at dance halls or theaters.

The earliest vaudeville performances were in halls that were loud and boisterous and often served alcohol. During the 1890s, much of vaudeville moved to "palace" environments that combined the gaudy beaux arts structures of Coney Island with the refined elegance of legitimate theater houses. These environments offered three tiers of seating separated by price. The laborers who could afford 10 cents literally sat on the floor. The downtown workers sat in the upper balcony for 20 cents. The upper-class theatergoers, paying the full 30 cents, were given the best seats directly in front of the stage on the main floor.

By breaking the audience up, the theater managers attracted both the middle class and the upper middle class. These theaters soon brought a broad representation of the entire "community" into the performance atmosphere. The spectacle of both the play and the environment attracted groups that might not have mixed socially in other environments, but felt comfortable in sharing the vaudeville entertainment experience.

THE INTRODUCTION OF MOTION PICTURES

Vaudeville's success lay in no small part in filling the growing leisure needs of town residents. Walter Eaton, writing for the *New York Sun* in 1908, explained away the lack of story lines that audiences often faced by the fact that these same audiences did not care as much about the quality of the show as about the opportunity of going out and escaping the home (qtd. in Nasaw 1993, p.41).

It was at this time that Edison began to license his kinetoscope to penny-arcade proprietors. As noted in chapter 1, the first kinetoscope parlor opened in New York on April 6, 1894. Penny-arcade proprietors understood that they were defining modern entertainment. Every element of the penny arcade was built to highlight the cutting edge in technology. However, the penny-arcades' success was short lived, and within weeks of the success of the Pittsburgh Nickelodeon in 1905, New York's streets began to see a proliferation of 5-cent theaters. The town went movie crazy. The white-collar working class was the primary group that made up the audience during these days. New York, helped by a daily influx of immigrants, became the world's capital of theaters.

THE ENTERTAINMENT DISTRICT CREATES A BACKLASH

The growth of theater districts contributed to the development of entertainment communities located in the downtown. Groups representing a wide divergence of economic and religious backgrounds got together and shared the common experience of a film and, in the process, participated in a sense of community that had not to this point existed.

New York, due to its size, had to deal with the effects of clashes in culture, religions and ethnic divisions. The introduction of films challenged the norms of the day, and with several million Americans in one city, the morality battles soon began. The growing popularity of the theater worried both politicians and church groups, who became concerned about the impact on the community from the uncensored infiltration of outside images. Within a year of the first nickelodeon theater, church leaders demanded that local principalities shut down the movies and institute censorship codes. They were increasingly concerned that images produced by filmmakers and exhibitors (who were often Jewish) not under their control would create ideas that threatened the moral and religious concepts they held dear.

If censorship battles were not enough, the 5-cent theater faced the same problem that the penny arcade had a few years earlier: boredom. Adolph Zukor remembered that audiences were becoming bored with the short films being shown (Irwin 1928, p.121). Despite attempts to make the small theaters interesting, the novelty of the short-film experience was beginning to wear off, and the audiences began to stay away from the theaters. Theater owners realized that they needed to do more than offer a movie. They had to attract the audience to a show and an environment that promised entertainment that would bring them back week after week. This called for re-inventing the theater into an environment of spectacle.

Chapter 4

Queen Elizabeth
and the Feature Film

Storefronts from coast to coast began converting to 5-cent theaters in unprecedented numbers, and audiences were drawn in by the novelty of the environment and the films being shown. Exhibitors realized, however, that this was but the first step in a growing business. The industry periodical *Moving Picture World*, created at the birth of the nickelodeon, predicted that change was in the wind. Writer Louis Reeves Harrison warned, "The little theaters and the bigger ones which have grown out of little theaters must keep pace with the times to hold present patronage and draw in the millions who have not yet acquired 'the habit'" (Harrison 1912, p.521).

One of these exhibitors was Adolph Zukor. By 1912, he had become a seasoned theater operator. Zukor's experience with exhibition began with vaudeville theaters as well as penny arcades. As described in chapter 1, when Hale's Tours came along, he discovered a new opportunity in motion pictures, opening several more Hale's Tours around the northeastern United States. But audiences soon stopped flocking in. His partner, William Brady, cautioned Zukor that the problem was offering a one-time gimmick. The idea of a train ride in the middle of the city was a novelty and lured people in off the street. However, once someone had seen the show, he or she did not want to return. Zukor rethought his concept and decided to rebuild his Hale's Tours as regular theaters, showing films with real story lines. Soon these theaters became profitable again.

Zukor went beyond his Hale's Tours experiment and began to operate larger theaters with such partners as Marcus Loew, future owner of the Loew's Theater chain and MGM Studios. In 1911, he struck out on his own and opened the Comedy Theater at 46 Union Square. This was a far cry from the small spaces of a few years back and was described by film historian Terry Ramsaye as giving a "reasonably good imitation of a regular theater" (1926, p.431). Zukor offered what most other film exhibitors showed: a series of one-reel shorts coupled with vaudeville acts if the films were not going to be strong enough on their own to bring in the audience.

Zukor, however, was never content with the status quo. He always believed that the feature-film industry had a long way to grow. In the back of his mind, he kept thinking about the fact that the legitimate stage theaters commanded $1.50 a seat in the orchestra, while his theaters were limited to a nickel. Something had to be done to make the presentation so interesting that theatergoers would be willing to pay more. He strongly felt that for the motion-picture industry to grow and for theaters to succeed, they had to offer stories that would last more than a few minutes. His model was the Broadway play, which he found offering a powerful story within a glamorous theatrical environment.

He began looking for a way to make his dream happen. One of his colleagues was Edwin S. Porter, the director of the first story-driven film, *The Great Train Robbery*. Porter informed Zukor of the opportunity of investing in a feature-length film that would star the greatest stage name of the day, Sarah Bernhardt. The play was *Queen Elizabeth*, and the film was going to be made in France by a director named Louis Mercanton. Zukor jumped at the chance of purchasing the American rights and invested the then hefty sum of $18,000.[1]

To many theater owners and distributors at the time, Zukor's move was plain insanity. The prevailing logic was that theatergoers would not want to sit through a 40-minute-long story. Zukor decided to visit Thomas Edison's Motion Picture Patents Company, the organization that controlled the licensing of motion pictures, and enlist its support. Zukor asked for a meeting with Jeremiah J. Kennedy, head of the company, for a license to show *Queen Elizabeth*. After Zukor waited for three hours to meet the company's president, Kennedy sat down with Zukor and told him in no uncertain terms that they were not interested in doing features, explaining, "The time is not ripe for features if it ever will be." Zukor later recalled that he did not take

Trade advertisement for *Queen Elizabeth* taken out by Adolph Zukor's Famous Players Film Company. *Moving Picture World*, August 10, 1912.

the three hour wait as intentional, since to the trust, he "wasn't considered important enough to justify discourtesy" (Zukor 1953, p.73).

To Edison's production and distribution company, Zukor became one more outlaw. He joined a growing list of producers and exhibitors who did not want to abide by the narrow vision that the trust had in the future of films. With the patent company showing no interest, he decided to open *Queen Elizabeth* himself. Using his vision of a Broadway presentation, he wrote to Charles Frohman, a leading stage producer in New York. Frohman did not share Zukor's vision either, but sent the letter over to his brother, fellow producer and theater owner Daniel Frohman.

Unlike his brother, Daniel Frohman was intrigued with the idea. He had recently sponsored the American appearance of Bernhardt and was open to an adventurous opportunity. Zukor met with Frohman in his apartment above the stage of his notable theater, the Lyceum in New York. Zukor shared his vision of feature-length films, films that exhibitors and audiences would pay more for since they offered a higher-class form of entertainment. Frohman decided to form a partnership with Zukor and offered the Lyceum Theatre for the first showing of *Queen Elizabeth*.

The Lyceum was an interesting choice. Built in 1903 by Frohman himself, the Lyceum had a seating capacity of 924 and offered the perfect environment to test the idea of a stage play in feature-length-film form. It was an elegant showplace, one that is still in use a century after it was built.

On July 12, 1912, Zukor created a series of milestones that would inspire decades of film presentations to follow. *Queen Elizabeth* ranks as one of the earliest feature-length films ever made, and its showing in a premier Broadway theater was a first. The Saturday matinee showing also was unprecedented. Zukor and Frohman described it as a "premiere" aimed at invited guests only. From this day on, the "film premiere" has become a unique community activity, one that brings the spectacle of the event outside the theater and into the street. Under the influence of Frohman's pull, the full house that showed up at the Lyceum was made up of New York's finest, many of whom made a special trip from their summer shore homes just to see the event.

The initial press response was less than earthshaking. The *New York Herald* wrote a review the next day, faulting the feature film's stodgy performances but commending Bernhardt for appearing in the feature-length presentation. *Moving Picture World,* waiting almost three months before it reviewed the film, carefully described it as one filled with "dignity and an unmistakable care in the preparation of every detail" (Bush 1912, p.428).

What the *Herald* and *Moving Picture World* did not report was the effect the show had on the minds of exhibitors at the time. A feature-length film shown in a Broadway environment spelled the future of the motion-picture theater. This fact alone, despite being missed by the press at the time, turned out to be the most unique aspect of the presentation. Just as news of the Nickelodeon in Pittsburgh soon spread around the country, exhibitors from coast to coast, many of them friends with Zukor, soon realized that presenting a feature would allow them to offer an entirely new level of entertainment—as well as increase their prices. They also were aware that patrons would expect a higher quality of theatrical experience for the added price. Within months, the dynamics of exhibition and the design of Main Street began to change. Nickelodeons started closing one by one as larger theaters began attracting audiences to the new feature-length shows. The simpler storefront theater gave way to works of fantasy, enticing the pedestrian to enter into another dimension of reality where time and space would magically change, the movie palace.

NOTE

1. Ramsaye said that the amount was $18,000 (1926, p.595). Zukor (1953, p.61) later said it was $40,000. Irwin gives the amount as $35,000 (1928 p.156). The facts of film history, even a few short years after the events happened, are often hard to corroborate.

Chapter 5

Palaces on Main Street

Within months of the *Queen Elizabeth* opening, the first movie palace opened, New York's 1,845-seat Regent Theatre. Built in 1913 and designed by architect Thomas Lamb, it was modeled after the Doge's Palace in Venice. The classic proportions and historical basis would give it instant recognition, both to those aware of its landmark inspiration and those who did not. The theater stood out on two counts: It was built outside the old Broadway theater district in a working-class neighborhood; and it was dedicated to movies, up to this point a rather novel concept. The elegance also tried to compete with local vaudeville houses for middle-class audiences. Unsuccessful at first, it finally drew audiences after being redesigned by an up-and-coming showman named Samuel Rothapfel, better known as Roxy.

As the telephone affected where people lived and worked and the trolley influenced their ability to travel greater distances than had been previously available, so the movie palace changed the way America developed its sense of community. As soon as movie theaters began spreading around the country, they helped introduce a new set of design standards, blending modernism with commercial accents, classic motifs and modernistic comforts.

The movie theater soon became the meeting ground for the city, and the experience of watching the film was equally matched by the

Temple Theater, Scottish Rite Temple. A melding of two worlds. Miami, Florida, January 29, 1926. (Courtesy of the Florida State Archives)

surroundings in the theater. The movies and the theaters they were shown in would change the design of the American cityscape. Every major city in the country demonstrated its growth and culture by the size and grandeur of its movie houses. Beginning in 1918, from coast to coast, film studios and private exhibition companies commissioned thousands of new palaces, and as the theaters appeared, so did the audiences. By 1930, attendance rose to nearly 90 million weekly (*Encyclopedia of Exhibition* 1998, p.235), and the cinema became the most successful form of mass-culture entertainment as well as mass socialization that America had ever seen. The growth in motion-picture exhibition helped create a society that utilized new technologies to create a novel entertainment community, one that Adorno and Horkheimer described as the culture industry (1972). The movie palace, which brought tens of thousands of moviegoers to newly invigorated "entertainment districts," also changed the look of the central business district. The theater marquee became one of the key icons that defined the physical layout of the American downtown and neighborhood shopping district.

The movie palaces, like the films that they featured, evolved over a period of two decades, from 1912 to 1930. They took their initial inspiration from the great live stage theaters in New York, such as the 5,000-seat Park Hippodrome. But the movie palace overwhelmed the early models by delivering the size combined with modern comforts, all at an affordable price.

As early as 1914, distributors realized that there were several classes of theater available and ranked them according to size and grandeur, from the newest palatial theaters in prime areas to older, smaller theaters in out-of-the-way locations (Stones 1993, p.31). By the early 1930s, theater exhibition had proven itself as a viable business opportunity. Seven standardized formats became available, depending where one was building, how much one wanted to spend and what size the audience was ("Boeckh's Manual" 1998, pp.19–23).

The industry began to formally standardize its practices as the film-production companies controlled distribution of films. This allowed staged releasing, with the highest-price showings at the premiere runs in larger towns and the less expensive showings later in smaller towns.

Architects experimented with a host of styles that included Greek revival, Spanish baroque and Italian rococo, Egyptian pyramids, Gothic churches or Mayan temples. A combination of popular and highbrow culture created environments that were unique blends of each.

As the movie theaters grew more successful, they started to increase their proximity to the retail district. To help subsidize the cost of construction, the urban palaces began to combine functions, locating the theater on the bottom floors and building office structures above. In Los Angeles, for example, the original Orpheum, built in 1911, located itself in the heart of Los Angeles's business district and had retail establishments on the street level and offices above. The ornate structure, featuring classical revival exteriors, was meant not only to entertain and enthrall but also to attract a more middle-class clientele.

SPECTACLE ON MAIN STREET

The motion-picture industry was temporarily set back by American involvement in World War I. When the war ended in 1918, the country once again saw a leap forward in the reshaping of downtown America. From 1914 to 1922, more than 4,000 new theaters were built in the United States. However, the numbers underestimate the real change on the street.

S. Charles Lee, architect and builder of nearly 250 palaces, used to say that "the show started on the sidewalk" (Valentine 1994, p.9). The movie may have been an excuse to come to the theater, but the entertainment experience began long before the show started. With thousands of people attending each show, life on the street changed as palaces began appearing on the landscape. The palace promised luxury and comfort, and the patrons soon began treating their theaters as they would their churches. In lines of audience members in the 1920s and 1930s, the dress style fit the opulence of the institution.

The earliest movie palaces may have found initial inspiration through the opera and Broadway playhouses, but it did not take long for the movie theater to find its own form. The palace experimented with a combination of sidewalk spectacle and interior lavishness coupled with creature comforts. Plush seats, organs and noiseless projection introduced the sense of "modern." A well-manicured staff of trained attendants made the moviegoing experience competitive with the finest opera for a price the working class could afford. Attendees were escorted to their seats and shown where to wait before the show, all in an environment that was meant to awe.

The combination of affordability, entertainment and spectacle created the community of the theater in the central business district. The movie palace mimicked in many ways the functioning of a house of worship, and for the new leisure class, the film became the object of devotion. The city, through the emerging entertainment districts, had an affordable yet opulent public meeting place that was open for all to share, whether one was rich or poor, Protestant, Catholic or Jewish, a child, a single woman or a retiree. The only limitation was the color of one's skin, an important distinction that would define American communities for decades to come. This was a church without a denomination, a government building without the cares of democratic regulations. It was an urban realm in which the world became composed of an immense accumulation of spectacles. The movie palace created a world of affordable luxury the likes of which Americans had never seen before.

Chapter 6

Roxy

On April 12, 1914, less than two years after the premiere of *Queen Elizabeth*, the New York Strand Theatre opened its doors. What made this theater unusual for its time was that it was not a movie house converted from a storefront, but was purposely built as a movie palace patterned after the great Broadway theaters and located on Broadway at 47th Street. The Strand, built by Mitchell Marks, a former partner of Zukor, offered moviegoers an experience unlike any theatergoers had ever had before.

Horace Fuld, writing for the January 14, 1914, *New York Dramatic Mirror* described the theater as the "largest and most elaborate moving picture house in New York," with nearly 3,500 seats, and offering the latest in technologies that would allow for a comfortable moving-picture-going experience, including "the latest patent ticket-selling machines and the latest ideas of light and ventilation" (p.54). Marks had installed a ventilation system that constantly circulated warm air in the winter and cold air in the summer, with mushroom valves under the seat and ventilators in the side walls. Among what were considered innovations at the time, the theater had a two-story rotunda and mezzanine promenade in the front of the house and semi-indirect self-suffusing lighting, both firsts for motion-picture theaters. The stage contained a smaller stage for motion-picture presentations, including a large fountain, allowing for live shows as well as films. The Strand's sense of spectacle was largely the work of the theater's manager, Samuel R. Rothapfel, better known as "Roxy."[1]

Roxy further refined the spectacle environment, adding a cosmetic suite for theatergoers, a hidden orchestra and Pullman lounge seats in a room supported by Corinthian columns, all for a quarter's admission. The palace had suddenly become designed to define spectacle, with historical themes intermixed with modern luxuries. Attending the Strand was very much like going to a presidential reception or the first night at an opera. The Strand made the point that this was a location that one had to visit.

Roxy's career began in 1908, when the traveling salesman and ex-marine walked into a tavern in Forest City, Pennsylavania. Rothapfel fell in love with the owner's daughter and decided to stick around town. In an attempt to ingratiate himself with the tavern owner (and eventual father-in-law), he began working there and soon came up with an idea for the underutilized dance hall on the second floor. Rothapfel had seen the success of nickelodeons around the country in his travels and decided to convert the space to a movie house. What set him apart was his vision of a movie house. He papered the town with promotion notices, and when patrons arrived, they discovered a unique experience: Rothapfel had created a multicolored light show accompanied by background music. This was the first stage of what would become a career of theater management. He spent the next several years developing his talents in motion picture presentation. In 1912, he was hired to make a financially failing Milwaukee vaudeville house, the Alhambra, into a successful motion-picture institution.

Roxy received this commission shortly after Zukor's showing of *Queen Elizabeth* by convincing the Alhambra's owner, Herman Fehr, that feature-length photoplays were the means to success. A dubious Fehr trusted Roxy's lead, and Roxy redesigned the Alhambra from a nondescript vaudeville theater into one of the earliest prototype movie palaces. Roxy understood that the public wanted to be pampered. They wanted to experience the exotic. Entertainment did not simply begin on the screen, but was at the heart of the moviegoing experience. He put in a nursery in the back for young children. The theater was newly draped and had theatrically appointed lights and new carpets installed. Ushers were hired, and uniforms were designed for them. An orchestra pit was created surrounded by a Japanese garden. When the theater opened, it became an instant success, and the exhibitor was realizing a profit within the first week (Hall 1961, p.185).

Roxy continued his success in converting old houses to new film theaters that surrounded the audience with an environment of fantasy. He brought the Parthenon to New York's Broadway in the guise of the Rivoli. The New York Rialto Theatre, built in 1916, featured an electric front sign that showered sparks and depicted an eagle flapping its wing. The spectacle was the attraction that brought thousands of people a day, benefiting not only the theater, but also the retail stores and restaurants that surrounded the entertainment district.

After 15 years of renovating and experimenting in designing movie palaces, Rothapfel had the opportunity to build his dream palace, unsurprisingly named the Roxy. Roxy had visualized the quintessential movie theater, described as the world's largest cinema, with seating for more than 6,300 people. It was nicknamed the "Cathedral of the Motion Picture" and both in its interior and exterior design was made to impress. On its opening night of March 11, 1927, the theater, built on the site of old car barns, revitalized the entire neighborhood by adding an unrivaled Gothic revival masterpiece cinema. Theatergoers of the day were treated to an evening that featured an orchestra, dancers and an army of ushers in a theater with its own hospital and library, a broadcasting room, state-of-the-art air conditioning, a stage

Roxy Theatre, 1944. Ushers being reviewed before the audience enters the theater. (Courtesy of the Library of Congress)

Interior of the Roxy, 1928. (Courtesy of the Library of Congress)

that had no equal and a sound system for the Vitaphone talking-picture system.

W.W. Ahlschlager, the theater's architect, pointed out that not only did it hold nearly 6,000 seats, but had standing room for more than 3,000 within the foyer. With three shows a day, the Roxy not only stood out as a monumental design, but also was instrumental in changing the transportation and sidewalk usage of the area surrounding the theater as upwards of 18,000 people came through its doors daily.

The construction of the Roxy occurred at the penultimate moment of the movie palace. Within two years of the Roxy's opening, movie palaces began a gradual decline. There is no one villain, no one social or economic effect to blame, but a number of factors can share responsibility. First, the studios and theater chains had been overly optimistic in their construction plans and had simply built too many palaces. Even though an estimated 90 million Americans were going to films weekly, there were still too many theaters to go around. The Depression was also beginning in the United States, and movie attendance started to decline.

If these problems were not enough, Americans began to appreciate different architectural styles. While substantially fewer new theaters were built during the 1930s compared to the 1920s, the ornate classical styling of most palaces was replaced in popularity by the sleek lines offered by art deco theaters. The classic movie palace represented a bygone age, a failed era of borrowed and often gaudy representations. The American mood of 1930 was one desiring hope and looking forward to a brighter future, hopes mirrored in the modernistic designs that art deco represented.

Despite the Depression and World War II, the Roxy kept its doors open for the best part of three decades. However, it finally could not face the combination of the decline in moviegoing, a deteriorated interior and the demands of urban renewal. Despite the efforts of a concerted protest movement, it was torn down in 1961.

NOTE

1. Roxy's name appears in Ramsaye (1926) as Samuel Rothafel. In the April 12, 1914 issue of *New York Times*, it is spelled Sameuel R. Rothapfel.

Part Two

The Theater as a Mirror
of Society

Chapter 7

Colored Theaters

The problem of the 20th century is the problem of the color line.
—W.E.B. Du Bois

For the first decade after the opening of the Pittsburgh Nickelodeon, the country exploded with movie theaters. From coast to coast, in big cities and small towns, thousands of theaters were built. America embraced the new art form and seemingly could not have enough of it. However, along with this success came its fair share of conflict. The motion picture as well as its exhibition served as a mirror, reflecting the major events and social conditions of its day, both on screen and off.

In their classic study of middle America conducted during the 1920s, Robert and Helen Lynd discovered that Muncie, Indiana, had been profoundly affected by the movie theaters' relatively quick but ubiquitous appearance in town. With a total of 38,000 residents (Lynd and Lynd 1929, p.510), Muncie had nine theaters that operated seven days a week, from 1 P.M. to 11 P.M. The Lynds discovered that nearly 3 times the entire population of Muncie attended the theaters during July 1923, rising to more than 4 times the town's total population in December of that year.

Who went to the films? The Lynds discovered an economic divide, with only 3 of 40 business-class families avoiding the cinema while

The Gem Theatre was just one of several hundred segregated theaters in the country. Waco, Texas, 1939. (Courtesy of the Library of Congress)

38 of the 122 working-class families in the study avoided the motion-picture theater. The Lynds found that, as today, the teenagers in town were the most active moviegoers, with more than 70 percent of the boys and girls in high school going weekly to the theater, and a sizable group going three or four times a week. The audiences were generally interested only in entertaining films and avoided anything that seemed educational. One of the biggest theatrical failures in the local theater market was the Yale University Press's historical film series, which was cancelled after one week. However, films featuring Douglas Fairbanks, Sr., Gloria Swanson and Mary Pickford were eagerly sought. Many of the youngsters flocked to the 1923 production *Flaming Youth*, largely drawn in by the advertisements that promised "neckers, petters, pleasure-mad daughters and sensation-craving mothers" (Lynd and Lynd 1929, p.505).

Muncie was similar to most of America's community of cinemas. The theater became the principal form of community gathering, open to all age groups and economic and ethnic backgrounds, with one exception: black Americans.

By the early 1920s, Muncie was a town governed by a set of socially accepted racial standards. Only 30 years before, there had been little evidence of exclusionary social behavior among town residents, but by the 1920s, with an active Ku Klux Klan presence in town, Jews were forbidden to join the Rotary or country club and blacks were forbidden from the larger movie houses, YMCA, YWCA and "white" churches.

A SEGREGATED AMERICA

If one word defined the living and working conditions of black Americans around the country at the turn of the century, it must be segregation. After the 1896 *Plessy v. Ferguson* Supreme Court decision that upheld the principle of separate but equal, the social structure of America turned increasingly segregationist, with a strong embrace of "separate" and a short-term memory for the "equal."

The Supreme Court decision allowed a dramatic increase in segregationist legislation in the South that made it more and more difficult for black Americans to survive. As one gentleman complained, "They are Jim Crowin' us down here too much. There is no chance for a colored man who has any self-respect"(Ray Stannard Baker, in DeNevi and Holmes 1973, p.267). Unfortunately, the situation in northern cities was not appreciably better. Black Americans found despicable living conditions, with death rates higher than birth rates in towns such as Indianapolis (Baker, in DeNevi and Holmes 1973, p.265). Even in the seemingly more racially tolerant northern states, many smaller towns would not permit black Americans to stay overnight at hotels or inns.

Despite these conditions, black populations continued to flee the oppression in the southern states and moved to larger northern towns such as Philadelphia, New York and Boston. Along with the migration came increased segregation. By 1907, it was reported in Boston that several hotels, restaurants and confectionary stores would not serve black Americans. Even Harvard University, which had a tradition of integrating students, became largely segregated by the early 1900s (Baker, in DeNevi and Holmes 1973, p.271).

In the South, Jim Crow laws made it illegal for whites and blacks to congregate, whether it be at drugstore counters, buses, parks or movie theaters. In Atlanta, a series of laws created separate prisons, separate courts and even separate Bibles. Saloons, in which blacks and whites just a few years before had sat next to each other, were now segregated (Baker, in DeNevi and Holmes 1973, p.225). The laws were backed by a racist group of politicians who pushed the segregationist agenda as far as possible. In Atlanta during the early 1900s, the new public library system was ordered by the local government to serve "whites only." When the Carnegie Fund made it known that it was willing to pay for a "Negro branch library," the city would not allow its construction, even though it was not contributing the land or the finances. This was an America, according to W.E.B. Du Bois, in which "white people on the whole are just as much opposed to Negroes of education and culture, as to any other kind, and perhaps more so. Not all whites, but the overwhelming majority" (Paschal 1971, p.xxvii).

This was also the world that the nickel theater was born into. It is not surprising that colored theaters became the accepted norm throughout the entire South. In the North, local ordinances may have technically forbidden segregation, but northern theater owners created their own house rules. Many theaters were segregated by the neighborhoods they were built in. Others created their own form of segregation by developing two tiers of seating, with the expensive orchestra seats costing more than the affordable balcony seats. Sometimes the racism was blatant, with black customers being told that seats were not available, while white customers further back in line were able to purchase seats (Nasaw 1993, p.49).

The first-class theaters often had segregationist policies in place, regardless of one's ability to pay for seating or the illegality of the rule. While many of these theaters were picketed over time, many theater owners rationalized the practice by pointing to their customers and saying that they were only doing what the audience wanted.

Segregation had existed in neighborhoods, in the armed forces and in the retail districts throughout America for decades. However, the segregation that took place in the growing amusement culture of motion pictures had no precedent. Tens of millions of Americans went to the cinema weekly beginning in the second decade of the twentieth century, and a significant amount of them accepted segregation as part of their pursuit of entertainment. The racism developed as the theater developed, creating a secondary marquee that pronounced theaters as either closed to African Americans or exclusively colored.

As the nation's public places became more and more inaccessible to black Americans, it became increasingly common to challenge the practices. W.E.B. Du Bois reported several incidents of lawsuits in the NAACP magazine, *Crisis,* but despite occasional court victories, the policies seldom changed. In fact, segregated theaters became more and more prevalent in the decade during which nickelodeons and early palaces began to dominate the countryside, a practice not limited to the United States.

While the motion-picture theater was a new public space, much of its social behavior was learned from the established live stage houses. From the earliest days of vaudeville that predated film, African Americans were often restricted to sitting with prostitutes and their customers in the upper balcony, forced to enter via side doors or completely forbidden from attending (Nasaw 1993, p.49).

The vaudeville theater had a racist orientation not only in its seating policies but in the entertainment it offered. Vaudeville often featured white men in blackface and comedy that was demeaning in tone and purpose. With the vaudeville theater as inspiration, the earliest nickelodeon theater owners began to segregate audiences. Segregated audiences were not limited just to the South, however. It was part of the show, so to speak, in theaters throughout the country for the first six decades of the twentieth century.

The segregated audience created two communities of the cinema, one black and one white. They were soon divided not only by their seats, but also by different theaters, different films and bitter hatred. The theater's segregation helped define the future suburban communities that shared similar boundaries, allowing mixed religious and economic groups to live side by side—as long as they were not black.

On screen, the symbols of culture were mostly white, devoid of poverty, and economically challenged individuals or problems of society were most often ignored. African Americans, as well as other minority groups, were typically shown on the one hand as comic relief and on the other as dangerous characters. These characterizations rarely challenged the community norms, allowing films to have racist content but not face local censorship problems.

In what became known as "race cinema," colored theaters began showing films produced by black film-production companies. Between 1918 and 1950, more than 150 production companies were formed that specialized in the production of films composed of black casts for black audiences. However, the majority of these production companies were in existence for only a short time. Most were underfinanced and by the early 1930s were no longer in business or were under the control of a larger studio. Colored theaters for the most part had to resort to playing "white films."

In a 1929 survey of theaters across America, *The Film Daily Yearbook* inadvertently created a picture of segregationist attitudes city by city throughout the country. Hundreds of colored theaters dotted the countryside, located in both the smallest American towns and the largest cities. The survey pointed out that cosmopolitan cities such

Dixie Theatre, Appalachicola, Florida, 1951. A segregated neighborhood theater in a segregated community. (Courtesy of the Florida State Archives)

as New York had 10 colored theaters, while Boston, Denver, Des Moines, Portland, Pittsburgh, Seattle and Salt Lake City were without a single colored house, creating a mirror of the racial tolerance as well as the integrated populations of the various communities.

A FURTHER DIVIDE

It should not be surprising that the content of films would mimic the racism found in the audiences. From the earliest days of motion pictures, racist images were part of motion-picture entertainment. Edison's production company produced such memorable racist classics as *Cohen's Fire Sale*, in which a caricature of a Jewish clothing salesman burns his store down so he can collect the insurance. Children were entertained by such cartoons as *Piccadilly Days*, which glorified the southern tradition of slavery, showing dancing and singing slaves picking cotton.

In 1915, the separation of audiences in theaters entered the national spotlight with the distribution of a film that to this day is synonymous with racist cinema, *The Birth of a Nation.* The movie, directed by D.W. Griffith and based in part on Thomas Dixon's notoriously racist novel *The Clansman,* told the story of the birth of the Ku Klux Klan in the South and depicted African Americans as lazy, shifty, dangerous and evil.

The Birth of a Nation was shown in two parts. The first was focused on the final days of the Civil War, and its battle scenes have gone down in history as remarkable for the cinema of its day. Griffith's powerful direction and Billy Blitzer's camerawork combined to set a new standard for on-screen action and scripting. The second part, however, focused on the Reconstruction period and reflected the prejudices written in Dixon's book. Blacks, often played by white actors in blackface, were shown to be lusting after white women and feebly attempting to "play" legislators. The Klan was portrayed as the body that rescued the South from the conditions created by Reconstruction.

The Birth of a Nation has gone down in history as having succeeded in accomplishing a series of firsts, including being the highest-grossing film of its time and charging the highest amount for a seat ($2), as well as being the highest-attended film of its day. President Woodrow Wilson screened the film in the White House and exclaimed that it "was like writing history with lightning." The Supreme Court also had a personal screening, with Chief Justice Edward White, a former Klan member, particularly fascinated by the story (Rogin 1994, p.251).

Despite its success at the box office, *The Birth of a Nation* is considered to be one of the most censored films of all time. It was picketed in theaters throughout the United States, where inflamed demonstrators, both black and white, condemned not only the film's inherent content, but the fact that many of the black demonstrators were not even allowed to buy tickets and go in the theaters. Upon its initial release, the film faced more than 100 demands by groups promoting an end to segregationist policies in America. The battles against the film, many of which demanded its complete withdrawal from screenings, occurred both in and out of court. As the film went from select screenings in the major coastal cities to a general release across America, exhibitors were faced with legions of picketers who demanded that it be withdrawn.

The film industry was toeing a thin line between free-speech rights and censorship boards. The industry had prided itself in self-monitoring film producers and exhibitors. However, the idea of self-censorship was always aimed in fact at showing films that the public wanted and avoiding government intrusion. In the end, the film industry itself did not act decisively in limiting *The Birth of a Nation* from being shown. Despite the protests and the lawsuits, few local municipalities banned the film. President Wilson and Supreme Court Justice White, attempting to revise their earlier support of the film, publicly began to distance themselves from it.

Regardless of the outcry against its racist sentiments, *The Birth of a Nation* went on to be the biggest and most successful release not only of its day, but for years to come. Its success only further demonstrates the scope of racist sentiments of the day, sentiments that were reflected not only on the screen but in attendance at the theaters themselves.

Chapter 8

The Church Takes up the Fight against the Movies

No sooner had the nickelodeon craze begun to sweep the country than churches from coast to coast united in one common reaction: disgust. Church elders became fearful that church attendance would plummet commensurate with the increase in film attendance. Many municipalities put laws in place that forbade theaters to be open on Sundays, and religious leaders often sat on local censorship boards, cutting any offensive scene from films intended to be shown in their local theaters.

As soon as nickelodeons began to appear, they were criticized as being "demoralizing in their nature," especially upon the minds of children. The 5-cent theater was charged with being dangerous to public morals and paving the way to ruin for susceptible young children (*Moving Picture World*, May 11, 1907, p.148). The editors of *Moving Picture World*, the film industry's first weekly magazine, tried to rebut these charges:

The remedy for the evils of the five-cent theater is the same as that successfully employed in many other cases—the substitution of the wholesome and harmless for the unwholesome and hurtful. The five-cent theater has probably come to stay, as it has gained great popularity. This being so, entertainment of this sort that is lively, interesting and clean should be made as easily accessible as those of the other class. It will not do to make them dull or goody-goody. Persons in search of amusement, whether old or young do not want something dry and uninteresting forced upon them. Instead, they want life, action, fun and plenty of it. (*Moving Picture World*, May 11, 1907, pp.147–148)

The industry pep talk did little good. On April 23, 1907, only months after the opening of the first nickelodeon in Pittsburgh, the movie theater began to be perceived as a public nuisance in the largest city of the United States: New York. Police Commissioner Bingham called upon all commanders to create a "list of places of amusement in their jurisdiction, especially noting penny arcades and cheap theaters" (*Moving Picture World*, May 11, 1907, p.137). The action was brought by the city's health and fire departments out of concern that these establishments were a menace to society. At a meeting of the Board of Aldermen, a resolution was passed that demanded a complete investigation of the moving-picture craze:

There are to-day in existence throughout the city of New York various show places commonly known as "penny vaudevilles," "5-cent theaters," "moving picture shows," etc. all apparently being con-

YOUNG AMERICA AND THE MOVING-PICTURE SHOW.

Circa 1910 image showing children leaving church and going to a motion-picture theater, which leads them to a life of crime. (Courtesy of the Library of Congress)

ducted without complying with the provisions of part 21 of the Building Code, relating to public buildings, theaters and places of assembly, and particularly section 109 of said part of the Building Code, defining entrances and exits, seating capacity, width of aisles, fire precautions and matters of detail of building construction conducive to safety of life. (*Moving Picture World*, May 11, 1907, p.137)

The officials in New York may have tried to point to the building-code violations as being the problem, but the fact is that many citizens in New York were up in arms about movie theaters. They did not like the fly-by-night nature of many of the establishments, the types of people hanging out in front of the theaters and the crowds that were attracted to areas that once had been less populated. The Board of Aldermen declared:

These places of public entertainment have caused much annoyance and vexation to residents in their immediate vicinity, prompting the general opinion that they are a common nuisance, because of the gathering of motley crowds, and making of loud noises and breeding fear of disturbances and the danger of fires, of which one of a serious nature occurred in one of these places recently. (*Moving Picture World*, May 11, 1907, p.137)

The end result was that New York closed all its theaters for a short period to conduct inspections. The theaters that were up to code resumed operations, but this would not be the last time that officials in New York attempted this recourse to deal with the problems of 5-cent theaters.

The *Moving Picture World* also reported several theater owners attempting to placate churches and town officials. The management of the Nickeldom Theatre in Des Moines, Iowa, tried to make a distinction "between the clean moving pictures and other attractions and cheap, vulgar, sensational and morbid attractions in the Chicago 5-cent moving picture shows against which the *Chicago Tribune* is waging a vigorous warfare" (May 11, 1907, p.136).

For the next several years, motion-picture theaters tried various other techniques to get along with both cities and churches. In New York, manager Ed White of Weber's Theatre came up with the idea of "Church Film Parties." On May 27, 1912, his theater was turned over to the congregation of the Church of the Divine Inspiration, and the week before, the Church of Alliance also held a church-sponsored movie party ("Ed. White's" 1912, p.917).

Despite all attempts, the ruckus did not die down. Over the next several years, cities and churches continued their challenge to motion-picture theaters, with the discussion focusing on the moral damage that the theaters threatened in the community. In July 1912, the church group of the South Park Salem Lutheran Church debated the topic popular in the nation that year, "resolved, that the nickel theaters have done more injury to the church than the saloons." Their discussion was fueled by a recent court decision in which a judge had found a nickel theater owner guilty of the "Sunday Violation"—showing films on the Sabbath—at which time the judge charged that moving pictures were indeed worse than saloons ("The Picture" 1912, p.221).

The Sabbath laws were a difficult problem for early exhibitors, especially since Sunday was turning out to be one of the most popular filmgoing days of the week. In Hudson County, New Jersey, Greenwood Robinson was arrested for violation of the Vice and Immorality Act by reason of having shown films on Sunday. The case went to Judge Robert Carey, who did not challenge the appropriateness of the vice laws on the books but mentioned in his decision that "thousands of people in a community like Hudson County get practically no time for recreation except on Sunday and on holidays. Such people should unquestionably be legally accorded full opportunity to get some of the pleasure in life that a healthy kind of recreation affords." He pointed out that church could not take up the entire day, and that a large portion of the community was in favor of permitting the operation of such exhibitions. With his points well defined, but not wanting to challenge the existing law, he threw out the charge on a technicality ("Opinion" 1912, p.221).

In many ways, the early motion-picture film industry and the churches could not understand each other. Exhibitors and producers saw themselves as providing "good entertainment for the whole family and at a price which places that entertainment within the reach from one to six or seven times a week of all but the very poor." In fact, they saw film as a way to lure the men from the "back rooms of the saloon" into the presence of wholesome entertainment ("The Picture" 1912, p.917).

What the filmmakers could not address was the real underlying concern of churches: competition. Church leaders saw another gathering spot in the community that was attracting numbers equal to, if not greater than, those of people attending churches. Up to this point, the churches had had no real competition in their own communities. To add insult to injury, many of the theaters were fly-by-nght operations often run by Jews with film companies supplying films produced by Jews. The relationship would stay testy at best for years to come.

In *Middletown*, the Lynds reported that the Town Ministerial Association challenged the showing of "Sunday movies" in the fear that they would cut into church attendance (Lynd and Lynd 1929, p.269). Practical considerations may have taken precedence over spiritual worship, as the movies served as the ideal babysitter, with parents glad to have a safe place to put their children during a normally quiet day. Children who were forbidden to go to the movies on Sunday often complained to their parents that they were ostracized at school since they did not know what happened at the films and could not share in the discussions until later in the week. The events in *Middletown* were being repeated throughout the country. The movies became a driving force to create a secularized Sunday holiday out of the previous generation's Sabbath.

Church leaders were not the only ones to see the correlation between a religious house of worship and a place that allowed fans to worship their screen idols. Theaters shared much in common with the function of the church. An audience came regularly and sat in row seating. The films served as the information giver, with many of the early films including spiritual themes. As the theaters became more ornate, they took on the feel of large cathedrals and churches. It was no accident for Samuel Rothapfel to refer to his enormous Roxy Theatre as a "cathedral" to the motion picture. The church and movie theater had not found a way to co-exist.

Chapter 9

Crisis at the Box Office

Roxy was not alone in understanding how to please an audience. Three thousand miles away from New York, Sid Grauman was devising his own recipe for a successful theater, and he can arguably be called Samuel "Roxy" Rothapfel's West Coast kindred spirit. Grauman, like Roxy, started his career early in the nickelodeon days with the Unique Theatre in San Francisco. After developing his skills, he moved to Los Angeles and began building some of the largest theaters in the West Coast. Grauman may not have used cathedrals as his inspiration, but he took great pains to capture the spectacle—soaring ceilings and immense pipe organs—that large churches often offered. He was not shy about tying the reference to Grauman's "Cinema Temple."

In 1918, Grauman opened the Million Dollar Theatre in the heart of Los Angeles's developing movie district. Just to the right of the entrance was the descriptive explanation, a "temple to the cinema," which it very much was. The 2,350-seat Million Dollar was the largest house on the West Coast at its time, offering the most advanced ventilation system available and a stage area that was also large enough for both vaudeville plays and motion pictures. Sid Grauman eventually went on to help change the way Americans celebrated their movie-going experience. Ironically, the Million Dollar Theatre eventually became a church when the Broadway entertainment district's theaters began losing their clientele in the 1960s.

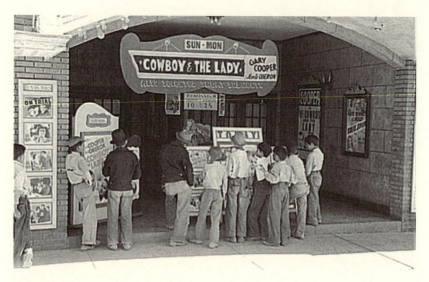

Children enter matinee performance, Alpine, Texas, 1939. (Courtesy of the Library of Congress)

In July 1927, Sid Grauman opened what was to become one of the greatest and longest-lived movie palaces in America, the Chinese Theatre in Hollywood, California. Invoking the religious connotation movie palaces were taking on, the reporters covering the palace's opening described it as the "Temple of the Cinema." It is somewhat ironic that the first film premiered at the new house was Cecil B. DeMille's *King of Kings*.

During the next six months, more than 500,000 patrons came to the Chinese to watch DeMille's classic story of Christ. With thousands of attendees coming nightly, the Grauman Chinese transformed Hollywood Boulevard. It brought in diners for restaurants and shoppers for retail establishments like the Broadway Department Store a few blocks away.

The Chinese promised entertainment not only in its auditorium but also on Hollywood Boulevard in front of the theater, and Grauman was the king at providing just such evening festivities. For Grauman, the show was not just about the movie. It was about the experience of going to the movie, which included waiting for the movie as well as the movie itself. His theaters, starting in 1918 with the Million Dollar Theatre on Broadway in downtown Los Angeles, were famous for their resplendent architecture and for the Grauman prologue. Tapping into the rich supply of vaudeville and silent-screen talent, Grauman produced prologues before each film that most often fit the theme of that evening's presentation.

Grauman's favorite hobby was collecting classic Chinese art, and his hobby became the inspiration behind a theater that can be described as a blend of neoclassical-meets-Mandarin architecture. After studying more than 20,000 photographs and drawings of Chinese architecture for inspiration as well as theater designs of buildings from coast to coast, he began construction of the theater with an estimated budget of five million dollars for the building and more than two million dollars in authentic artwork brought over from China.

Grauman was not content with simply offering a theater that stood out among his competition, or prologues famous from coast to coast. He created the art of street theater with the movie premiere. The Chinese Theatre has been home to more than 100 premieres since 1927, with one standing out as possibly the crowning moment in the community of cinema.

On May 27, 1930, aviator and movie producer Howard Hughes chose the Chinese Theatre to premiere his long-anticipated epic *Hell's Angels,* starring Jean Harlow. The community of cinema celebrated itself as a reported 150,000 Angelenos crowded into and around the blocks of Grauman's Chinese Theatre to watch the festivities.[1] Reserved seating ran an astronomical $11 a ticket, and advertising promised "a thousand movie stars" who planned to attend the premiere. If that were not enough, Grauman orchestrated an aerial show above Hollywood Boulevard to entertain the masses. The crowd outside swelled with anticipation, creating near-riot conditions that police were called in to monitor carefully. The events that night may have served as the inspiration for Nathanael West's novel *The Day of the Locust,* in which he renamed the Chinese "Kahn's Persian Palace" and described the crowds as "a veritable bedlam" (1933, p.86).

The crowds on the street watched aerial displays, and dozens of reporters brought the evening live to radio audiences around the country. The event outside ended as Jean Harlow made her way down streets guarded by police holding back the throngs in front of the theater and addressed the crowds. Harlow personally thanked Grauman for hosting the event as well as Howard Hughes for the opportunity of starring in the film. There has never been an event to equal the festivities that night.

The outpouring that evening may have been eagerly sought by Angelenos not only because of the spectacle promised, but as a way for many of them to avoid thinking about a situation they all faced together. The country was in the beginning years of the Great Depression, which at this point had not affected theater audiences.

THE CLASSIC STYLE IS OUT, ART DECO IS IN, AND EVERYONE IS GOING BANKRUPT

The community of the cinema was in high form at the end of the 1920s. The nation had an estimated 23,000 theaters in 1929, and an average of 90 million Americans out of a total population of 122 million went weekly to the movie theater.[2] The theater, along with the radio, newspapers and the telephone, had become the central means for mass communication in American society.

The undaunted growth in movie palaces would not go on forever. Within months of the *Hell's Angels* premiere, the film industry, along with its great movie palaces around the country, became a victim of the ever-increasing effects of the Great Depression. By early 1932, the Chinese Theatre closed its doors for several months, along with many other palaces in Los Angeles and around the country. Even some of the major studios like Universal and Paramount filed for bankruptcy.

During these years, movie-palace attendance dropped off from 90 million Americans a week in 1930 to 60 million by 1932 (Valentine 1994, p.195). Theater owners cut their admission fees, but in many cases it was too late. Movie theaters, which were overbuilt in the healthy economy of the early 1920s, began to close in unprecedented numbers across the country, dropping admission income from $720,000,000 in 1929 to $482,000,000 just three years later (*Encyclopedia of Exhibition* 1998, p. 235).

The cinema had to offer more if it was to win back its dwindling audience. Exhibitors and producers began studying their audience in greater detail than they had ever done before. They asked themselves what it would take to bring it back.

"WHEN IT CAME TO THEIR KIDS, PARENTS ALWAYS HAD A NICKEL"

While many of the major studios faced severe economic hardship during the early 1930s, one young entrepreneur named Nat Levine decided that the atmosphere was perfect to begin production. The founder of Mascot and Republic studios, Levine realized that Saturday mornings were reserved for the children, with matinees featuring serials and feature films—this was the world he wanted to own. Levine pointed out in a 1986 interview that Mascot studio thrived during the early Depression while others went bankrupt largely due to his production of serials aimed at Saturday morning matinees. Parents, he realized, would spend their last nickel on their children. Each Saturday morning, they would see the ongoing adventures of John Wayne; Gene Autry, the Singing Cowboy and Rin Tin Tin. Levine believed in low cost, high action and big names at bargain prices. He hired the aged Rin Tin Tin, for example, after he was "retired" from Universal. When the original Rin Tin Tin soon died, Levine introduced to his accepting audience Rin Tin Tin, Jr., which worked fine in his perspective for the average ten-year-old.

For evening adult audiences, theater owners began to devise a variety of techniques to attract customers, further changing the sense of community in Depression-stricken America. The theater managers realized that they needed to become a nexus for the community as they never had before. Spectacle had to go beyond the wonders of the theater's design. Spectacle had to touch the audience personally.

To this end, theater owners created a multitude of community offerings that changed the face of cinematic gathering. Theater managers were offered how-to guidebooks, such as *The Management of Motion Picture Theatres* (Ricketson 1938, p.189), which spelled out what theaters must offer to stay in business during the Depression. The suggestions would have much broader effects than attracting an audience. They would change the look and use of the retail districts during the Depression as well.

Suggestions included theater owners making their marquee readable from a distance to passers-by in streetcars and automobiles as well as street traffic. The marquee should be combined with banners and cutouts, creating a festive message that clearly announced the films and stars. Owners were called upon to make the lobby "the brightest spot in town."

The movies also became the home of a new brand of intensified advertising, commonly referred to as exploitation. The theater's events were not limited to the movie itself, but constituted an evening's entertainment that was guaranteed to be substantially out of the ordinary. Suddenly, towns across America could have their own "Shirley Temple bobs" contest or "Clark Gable look-alike" contest. Greta Garbo salads were featured at restaurants near the theater featuring her films. Mayors would issue proclamations tied to a film's theme, and newspapers would announce the arrival of Madame X, who could answer all questions before and after the showing of a film with a similar title.

The act of exploiting films became an art form, and studio publicists became expert at developing promotional campaigns that got wilder and wilder. Theater managers were inspired by such classic promotions as Paramount Studios' campaign for its feature film *Deception*, which included schoolchildren writing essays on the greatest deceptions in history, a merchants' campaign giving an award to the best store window exemplifying the least "deception" and local advertisers promoting their services by the assurance that they did not use "deception" in their newspaper ads.

As if these were not enough, exhibitors began to use special attractions to bring in the audience. Theaters offered a wide array of business stimulators, including the giveaway and games.

The giveaway had been part of small theater operations since the beginning of the nickelodeons, but by the middle of the Depression, its importance had grown substantially (Ricketson 1938). Many giveaways were not costly and included coupons from local businesses, but one stands out to define the period, and that was "Bank Night." This special occasion was a cash giveaway that helped lift the theater out of the bottom to which it had sunk in 1932 and literally added hundreds of thousands of new theater patrons. Bank Night inspired a multitude of other nights, all appealing to a wide divergence of audiences. Monday might be Bank Night, followed by Cash Night on Wednesday and Woman's Night or Plate Night on Thursday. Vaudeville acts, which had almost disappeared, suddenly reappeared in the hopes of offering cheer and more entertainment for the admission price. Theaters also created special events that might last several months, including car giveaways featuring a local car dealer's selections.

Games also became popular. Nearly 2,500 theaters began offering lotto, with cash, grocery and candy prizes. Popularity contests featuring babies, bathing beauties, mothers and athletes were held coast to coast. Impersonation contests and feats of skill were also tried, including contests that celebrated the cow giving the most milk and the largest family in the community. In Plainfield, New Jersey, Reade City Theatre manager Ed Hart promoted Fox's *Little Miss Marker* by offering a $25 reward for the best Shirley Temple look-alike. The July 1934 promotion included a girl in a costume who

Manos Theater, Elkins, West Virginia, 1939. "Plate Night at the Manos" was among the special incentive nights offered three times a week to help attract an audience during the Depression. (Courtesy of the Library of Congress)

resembled the starlet being paraded around town in an old-time carriage, and local papers encouraged parents to "test their child" in a ten-point rating by which they could see how much their children resembled little Shirley (*Motion Picture Herald*, August 11, 1934).

With Saturday morning matinees for the children and a multitude of special-event evenings throughout the week, the theater once again became a center of family and civic life. Many of the large theaters featured crying rooms so families could still watch the film, even with babies in hand. Managers were encouraged to know each regular customer by name and let these patrons know how important they were.

In the midst of this cultural rewriting of the rules that made up the relationship between movie theaters and their patrons, another major change was occurring in the environment of the theater itself. Patrons were less impressed with the classic palaces of the 1920s and more attracted to the modern look of the new art deco palaces that were taking shape during the 1930s. May (2000) has pointed out that the modernist theme was finding its way to all parts of the city, and the theater became part of this dramatic shift in the physical design of the urban atmosphere. While the grandiose thematic palaces gave way to modernistic structures, the theater did not lose its main draw, the guarantee that the environment would offer a feeling of spectacle, from the marquee outside to the lobby entrance and the actual seating area.

With the increased emphasis on events that brought the neighboring community together, movie theaters soon began to see a turnaround. Attendance began to rise, and by 1937 it was up to 88 million weekly and admission income rose to $676,000,000 (*Encyclopedia of Exhibition* 1998, p.235). The community of cinema, offering greater contact with patrons and reduced prices, became more than a movie event; it was the entertainment activity all Americans could afford.

NOTES

1. RKO Studios, in a trailer it produced for *Hell's Angels*, claimed a mind-boggling 500,000 fans.

2. Larry May challenges the industry numbers, claiming that they were inflated. For more information about his argument, see *The Big Tomorrow* (2000).

Chapter 10

Propaganda Wars

The motion-picture theater was not only an important community gathering spot, but a powerful environment to reach the hearts and minds of the American population. Even in the earliest days of motion pictures, the power of cinematic films became very obvious to both filmmakers and politicians. The popularity of short films produced about the Spanish-American War in the late 1890s was not lost on Washington, and the national furor created by *The Birth of a Nation* only intensified this awareness.

The federal government initially had a hands-off attitude regarding film. For the most part, decision making regarding the content of films was the responsibility of local and state government offices. However, when it became likely that the United States was going to be involved in the world war in Europe, the federal government became more active in using the cinema to reach out to mainstream America and explain the situation abroad. A cautious Wilson administration, not really knowing how to handle the intensity of the footage shot at the war front, began censoring most images of the war actually shot on the battlefield through the activities of the Committee on Public Information and the Creel Committee. (The committee, named after George Creel, was formed by President Wilson as a means of developing and disseminating propaganda to support the country's war efforts. It had the added power of the recently enacted

Sedition Act of 1918, which made many activities not supportive of the war effort illegal.) Along with censoring of images came the need to promote the cause of the war. Audiences attending movie theaters during the years of World War I were treated to world-famous stars such as Mary Pickford and Charlie Chaplin making filmed pitches to support the war effort. These film appearances were augmented

Promotional sheet for *The Road Is Open Again*. The song and a short featurette shown at theaters around the country attempted to develop popular support for President Roosevelt's National Recovery Act. (Author's collection)

by a group of speakers, known as the Four-Minute Men for the length of their addresses, who would personally encourage audiences to help in the war effort (Fielding 1972, p.123).

The American film industry attempted to maintain a pretense of neutrality as the war began. Most films dealing with the war focused on the violence and the inhumanity of the conflict. One notable propaganda film during this period was Thomas Ince's *Civilization*, which featured a reincarnation of Jesus Christ as a dead submarine engineer preaching the gospel of peace. Though the picture attempted to maintain neutrality, the uniforms and badges of the enemy forces were clearly German, reflecting the growing anti-German attitudes in the country.

In 1915, J. Stuart Blackton, producer of several Spanish-American War propaganda films, released *The Battle Cry of Peace*. Blatantly anti-German, the film was released at the same time that the *Lusitania* was sunk and further inflamed both the country's anti-German sentiment and the call to enter the war. The film showed Germans attacking New York and destroying its skyline, causing an inflamed and isolationist Henry Ford to take out numerous newspaper ads condemning the film. Ford's effort did little good, as the tone of other motion pictures produced at the time turned decidedly against Germay months before the United States actually entered the war.

As anti-German sentiment grew, so did the number of films that mirrored that sentiment. Cecil B. DeMille produced *The Little American*, featuring Mary Pickford being carried off by treacherous German soldiers. Other titles included *The Beast of Berlin* and *To Hell with the Kaiser!*

Typically, films that supported the war effort had no problem being shown in theaters. That was not the case for all war films during this period. For one producer, his film's content, as well intentioned as it was, caused him grave legal problems. In 1916, producer Robert Goldstein finished *The Spirit of '76*, which told the story of America gaining freedom from the British. The film was planned for release at the same time that President Wilson was about to help the British in the war against Germany. Not wanting to offend its allies, the U.S. government found the film to be dangerous to the war efforts. The film was banned from exhibition, copies were burned, and the producer was sentenced to ten years in prison under the 11th statute of the Code of Espionage.

Another director to face difficulties from an improperly timed film was D.W. Griffith. In 1918, Griffith and his two lead actresses, Lillian and Dorothy Gish, were brought over to England to create *Hearts of the World*, financed by the British government. The patriotic film dramatically showed the brutality of the Germans and was meant to inflame the public against the enemy. However, by the time it reached the screen in England, audiences had had enough of this form of war drama, and it had little popular effect. In America, it saw barely any distribution due to the fact that it was not available until the war ended, by which time the government was attempting to tone down the level of anti-German propaganda.

World War I was the first war that took advantage of a nation-wide community of thousands of cinemas. The mix of speakers, nationalistic propaganda shorts and feature films with patriotic themes would serve as the blueprint for the next world war, 25 years later.

WORLD WAR II COMES TO THE NEIGHBORHOOD THEATER

The year 1940 may have signaled an end to the Depression years only by the involvement of the United States in World War II. The movie theaters once again became an important pulpit in reaching

Neighborhood theater in Florida, circa 1943. During World War II, theaters served as an escape from the daily reminders of war. At the same time, theaters reached audiences with weekly updates about the war and the goals of the U.S. government. (Courtesy of the Florida State Archives)

Americans, explaining what the war was about and the need to fight. These were messages, however, that were not naturally conveyed by Hollywood producers and motion-picture exhibitors. In a warning to writers and producers, producer Sam Goldwyn has been credited with saying, "If you want to send a message, call Western Union." The film industry from its earliest days realized that controversy could lead to costly boycotts, local governments cutting up prints and federal government intervention. The early moguls instinctively understood that it was important to keep entertainment oriented to the mass culture and in 1922 hired conservative Postmaster General Will Hays to help guide the industry in that pursuit. Hays's mission was to stop local boycotts and keep the federal government out of films. Hays explained to the public in a 1930 newsreel, "A thousand hands would like to get their hands on motion pictures. They shall not. You want entertainment, and that is what the motion picture industry is pledged to provide!"

Despite Hays's wishes, creating films devoid of any underlying messages was difficult, especially during wartime, and the history of motion pictures has been in many ways defined by the battles over ideas. Given the immense power that the screen brought to messages inherent in scripts, it is no surprise that films became a means for the propagation of a doctrine or opinion.

With the coming of the Great Depression, many filmmakers looked at making the content of their films racier in hopes of attracting a wider audience. Church groups then became angrier, threatening major boycotts. The film industry once again looked to Will Hays to intervene and keep the protests from getting out of hand. He cracked down, hiring a tough lieutenant by the name of Joseph Breen to institute a very strict code of ethics. The 1934 restructuring of the motion-picture code under Breen mandated that the stringent list of dos and don'ts be accepted by all makers of American movies. The Association of Motion Picture Producers' code authority summed up the importance of the production code by pointing out that "the sympathy of the audience should never be thrown to the side of crime, wrongdoing, evil or sin" (*Motion Picture Herald*, August 11, 1934, p.11).

Breen's warning to producers actually made political propaganda much easier, as long as it was on the side of the American government. The industry was sending a message that it was supporting the government, and in turn Washington did not have to worry about creating national censorship standards. This was an important time for Hollywood to send that message, with the country in a depression and moralists such as Father Charles Coughlin charging that the film industry was ruining the country with its tales of crime and amorality (Lee and Lee 1939, pp.8–13).

Propaganda films that supported the New Deal and the National Recovery Act (NRA) began to appear on the nation's screens, produced not only by the U.S. government but by several Hollywood studios that attempted to maintain friendly relationships with Washington. One studio stands out as a major supporter of government efforts to invigorate the economy, and that is Warner Brothers. In shorts like *The Road Is Open Again,* actor Dick Powell explained the benefits to the country that the NRA would offer, singing its praises to lyrics written by one of Hollywood's greatest composers, Sammy Fain. Newsreels showed the efforts being made to rebuild the economy. Novice documentary filmmaker Pare Lorentz, avoiding the Hollywood system, took $6,000 in funding from the U.S. government and set out to record the effects of dust storms on the Midwest. The result was *The Plow That Broke the Plains* (1936), which graphically portrayed the plight of hundreds of thousands of Americans in the path of the storms and issued a call for improved conservation methods. The film was first ignored by Hollywood studios, but soon grew in reputation and eventually played in more than 3,000 theaters from coast to coast. It was followed by Lorentz's *The River,* a dramatic look at the effects of flooding on the Mississippi River. The power of the film was reflected by its positive effect on the public's acceptance of the government's regional work programs.

The Hollywood studios began to examine themes made popular in Lorentz's documentaries, and films such as *The Grapes of Wrath* were released. During this time, the deteriorating conditions in Europe were finding their way to story lines for films and newsreels that appeared on America's movie screens. For example, *Blockade* (1938) showed Henry Fonda as an American volunteer siding with the anti-fascists in Spain's civil war.

Despite several feature films with strong social themes, Hollywood in the late 1930s tried to stay neutral about the problems developing throughout Europe. It did not want to upset its European distributors nor raise any objections from Washington about involving itself in the affairs of governments with which the United States was technically still friendly. Feature films, cartoons and newsreels that deviated from this practice were censored from exhibition, a situation that

LO-SONS; LO-PARENTS!
More Sons-in-Service Club Members

Sgt. David Greenman, with his parents, LaVerne and Harry Greenman. Harry is the manager of *Loew's Theatre* in Pittsburgh, Pennsylvania.

Service trio: Cpl. Jos. Coco, left, SC 3/c Salvatore Coco, center, and Pvt. Alfred Coco, sons of Al Coco, projectionist, *Loew's 175th St.*, N. Y. Alfred recently received his honorable discharge from the U. S. Army.

SC 3/c Nick Carlance, Jr., son of Nick Carlance, poster artist, *Loew's, Theatre*, Reading, Pennsylvania.

Pfc. Felix P. Schuellein, Jr., and his father, Felix P. Schuellein of *News of the Day.*

F 1/c John J. Hackett, and S/ Sgt. Wm. M. Hackett, sons of John Hackett, engineer, *Loew's Grand*, Bronx, N. Y. C.

Cpl. Harry Blanchard, and his mother. His dad is Lyman Blanchard, painter, *Loew's Penn*, Pittsburgh, Pa.

Pvt. John Magnatta, son of Fred Magnatta, projectionist, *Loew's Prospect*, Flushing, at left with dad, right with mother. John was wounded on D-Day.

Bruce Allen Lance, U. S. Merchant Marine, son of Mrs. Mae Lance, matron, *National Theatre*, N. Y.

DI sons and parents above are: AMM 3/c Mervyn Shopenn; his mother, Minerva Shopenn, of the Home Office *Sales Dept.*; Lester Fritz, projectionist, *Loew's Granada*, Cleveland; his son, Pvt. Lester Fritz, Jr.; Wm. Mackay, doorman, *Granada*, Cleveland; his son, Lieut. Col. Jos. Mackay, Army Air Force; Nicholas Tedesco, projectionist, *Poli-Palace*, Hartford; and his son, Lt. William Tedesco. These pictures received since last issue of LO!

Loew Corporation's magazine saluted Loew's Theater employees and families in the service during World War II.

the newsreel series *March of Time* faced when it produced an episode about the militaristic plans of Adolf Hitler. The short was banned from being shown in the United States for fear that it would upset the German government (Barnouw 1974, p.121).

The propaganda battles may have begun due to moralistic concerns between the film industry, the government and various church groups, but they took an entirely new direction once World War II broke out and the United States was embroiled in the middle of the conflict. After Pearl Harbor, the country was entirely focused on war. The theaters took on several important tasks, including newsreels that showed the war on a weekly basis. The government encouraged films produced by the movie studios that explained who the enemy was and why the United States was fighting. Bond drives were held in theaters from coast to coast. Theater chains made a point of watching out for their own employees in the service. Loew's, with more than 2,200 workers fighting in Europe and in the Pacific, began organizing its Christmas presents in September. The "Loew's Christmas box" included one pound of chocolate candy, Jordan almonds, four tins of anchovies, figs, razor blades, shaving cream, a detective book and a cigarette lighter (*Lo Magazine*, October 1, 1944, p.3). The chain also made sure that films of MGM, a subsidiary of Loew's were sent overseas and required its employees to have bonds taken out of their paychecks weekly.

For the country as a whole, the movie theater offered a refuge, a sense of safety and security in a country that had gone through ten tough years only to face millions of its young men and women going overseas to fight. The movie theater was a weekly home away from home that safely brought the action on the homefront to the families wanting to have some sense of what their husbands, sons and daughters were going through. It also served as the best way that the United States government could explain what it was doing and why, keeping morale up during some very difficult years.

Part Three

Social Upheaval

Chapter 11

Cinema Goes to the Suburbs

At the war's end, the theater evolved to once again take on a new role in society. Throughout the country, the growing ideal of an American family life in the ever-expanding suburbs inspired both real growth outward and screen portrayals of suburban families shown in theaters that served the growing new community of cinema. Downtown theaters inevitably faced shrinking audiences.

As most cities began to expand outward, so did their entertainment needs. Neighborhood theaters began to be the acceptable choice, with automobiles giving theatergoers the freedom to go where they wanted. One form of theater that fit into the suburban neighborhood was the drive-in.

Richard Hollingstad, Jr., of Camden, New Jersey, first introduced the drive-in in 1933. It did not take long for his concept to raise considerable interest. However, since this was the middle of the Depression, theaters were lucky to simply stay open, and the popularity of the drive-in did not spread as quickly as Hollingstad had hoped. Over the next 15 years after the Camden opening, only 820 drive-in theaters opened from coast to coast. The Depression was not an easy period in which to revolutionize the screening of films and to incur the expense of new theater construction. However, after World War II, the drive-in caught on with a vengeance. In 1948, the country had 18,631 theaters, of which only 820 were drive-ins (*Encyclopedia of Exhibition*

Oaks Theatre, Berkeley, California. The Oaks was built in 1925 by the Reid brothers, and has served as a neighborhood movie theater ever since. (Author's collection)

1998, p.218). Four years later, in 1952, there were 3,276 drive-ins with room for 263,879 cars, compared to only 65 new indoor theaters built that year, offering less than 35,000 new seats. Nearly 3,000 indoor theaters closed during this same time (Segrave 1992, p.65).

The drive-in became the new symbol for the suburban entertainment district. It was popular because it offered the community what was needed in postwar America. America was in the midst of a baby boom. Families chose the comfort of a theater in their suburban community that offered a playground for the children and the privacy of their car over the comparatively challenging trip downtown with its commute and parking problems.

In one survey of drive-in audiences, commonly called "ozoners," 700 out of 1,286 responded that they would not have gone to the movies if they had had to go indoors. They went to the drive-in because of the convenience to their neighborhoods (Segrave 1992, p.143). With the growing accessibility of automobiles to teenagers, the drive-in became a rite of passage for millions of Americans during their adolescent dating. Drive-ins may have been banned in some conservative parts of the country, but they were phenomenally popular in most communities. For this very reason, by 1958, the number of drive-ins had risen to more than 4,000. The indoor theater, by comparison, continued to decline in gross numbers around the country (*Encyclopedia of Exhibition* 1998, p.218).

The drive-in offered family comfort while still supplying an environment of spectacle that the indoor palace had established. The drive-in's screen was upwards of five stories tall, becoming a landmark for the community in which it was located. The parklike atmosphere of the drive-in provided a playground for children, and snack bars that were patterned after amusement parks in their design and function. Most important, the audience, sitting in the privacy of their cars, stood as a metaphor for a paradigm shift in the style of community gathering. Thousands of moviegoers chose to sit alone in their cars rather than gather and sit directly next to strangers.

THE COMMUNIST THREAT COMES TO THE LOCAL THEATER

The movies during this period not only reflected the changes in societal living standards, but also the political tone of the day. The Cold War films mark in many ways the maturity of propaganda, politics and the motion picture. Hundreds of titles were released and shown in America's theaters that had subtle and sometimes not-so-subtle messages about the dangers of Communism, clearly marking the enemy as godless, evil and downright imperialistic. Whatever the story line may have been, the themes of the films were the same.

The propaganda campaign of the Cold War was waged on many fronts, but the cinema house was the primary pulpit. Newsreels in the late 1940s and early 1950s covered in earnest the House Un-American Activities Committee, making Senator J. Parnell Thomas a nationally recognized figure as he came to Hollywood in search of "Reds." The American film industry battled the Communist conspiracy in such films as *I Married a Communist*, *The Red Menace* and *I Was a Communist Spy for the FBI*. Even science-fiction films used the fear of Communism as inspiration for plot lines, with aliens with personalities akin to the Cold War vision of Communist government officials taking over human beings in *Invaders from Mars* (1953) and *Invasion of the Body Snatchers* (1956).

The threat of Communism was not shown only in feature films and newsreels. Through the efforts of Hollywood studios and the Department of Defense, a variety of short films were produced explaining the Communist threat to Americans. In *Crimes of Korea* (1951), narrated by Humphrey Bogart, Americans were shown grisly images of North Korean atrocities against the South in the early days of the Korean War. In *Face to Face with Communism* (1952), a documentary-style narrative explained how an army soldier awoke in a town where everyone had turned into a Communist. The soldier, fearing for his life, laments, "If it's a Communist world, I would rather be dead."

It was hard to go to the movies and not escape the propaganda battles that began in the late 1940s and continued through the early 1960s. The head of the Motion Picture Association of America, Eric Johnston, warned that all films should support the fight against Communism. "It is our everlasting hope that our motion pictures blend together to transplant before the eyes of others the shimmering spectral pattern that is America" (1950, p.11).

THE COMMUNITY OF SPECTACLE IN THE 1950s

As the suburban movement spread, the indoor theaters battled for their existence. From a postwar high of more than 19,000 screens in 1948, they began to close in great numbers throughout the country. By 1963, only 8,665 indoor theaters were still showing films. The rest had been torn down or reutilized.

Multitudes of improvements were attempted to stem the tide. Theaters began offering Coke in 1947 (Stones 1993, p.104). Three-D movies were introduced in which audience members wore glasses to watch films with a 3-D effect. Wide-screen film presentations like Cinemascope and Cinerama were offered, in which the theater's screen was literally enlarged, creating an image that occupied the entire front of the auditorium.

Despite various new technologies and performance attractions, the theater's evolution during the 1950s and 1960s witnessed the loss of its link to the spectacle environment and the center of community. Over the course of the 1960s, the theater evolved into a minimalist dream, composed of a square box housing candy, draped walls and cement floors. Even the name "multiplex" was more likely to be found in economic books, as opposed to the grandeur that "cinema," "palace" or "cathedral" insinuated.

The effort to save the community of the cinema of the past may have been simply doomed to fail. In addition to cars, parking problems, suburbs and drive-ins, there was the television. In 1945, the country had only 9 television stations and a handful of television sets. By 1950, 80 stations were on the air, and Americans had more than 3 million sets. By 1952, the number of stations had leaped to 2,000. The television, despite poor reception and commercials, was seen by post–World War II America as the new, modern marvel, and the public was mesmerized. The spectacle that once had been provided by the theater was now moving into the living room. The movie palaces, which had been shrinking in popularity since the late 1920s, could not compete with the novel attraction that the television and drive-ins offered teens and young families. They could not compete with smaller, more modern neighborhood theaters that offered easy accessibility and parking. Finally, the theater became part of a much bigger shift in retail shopping characteristics. The freedom that the automobile supplied and the flight of not only the theater, but the retail establishments from the downtown to the malls and suburbs was the final nail in the coffin for the downtown movie palaces.

THE AUTO AND THE MARQUEE

The theater marquee, which had developed into the street-level signature of the theater, soon began to take new forms as it grew to become a beacon for auto-driven theatergoers trying to find the location. Modern architecture combined with practical need in the creation of towers and signs that began to detail community, suburban theaters in the 1930s and 1940s.

By the early 1960s, the theater had denigrated itself to a minimalist box that Walter Gropius would have been proud of. Gone was any sense of ornate plastering, classical motifs or art deco style. The theater that evolved in the 1960s became a cubicle devoid of any ornate features, divided into smaller chambers in which the dwindling audience could watch the film of choice. It was invented more out of need than by design when theater owners realized that they could make more money showing two films in the same space with the same number of personnel as one theater took.

It was during the 1970s that the drive-in—a rite of passage for teenagers spanning nearly three decades—began to close nationwide. Malls began to attract the target audience away. Families did not attend in the numbers they had in the 1950s and 1960s. At the same time, land values skyrocketed, making the acreage the drive-ins occupied valuable pieces of property. By the end of the twentieth century, fewer than 800 still existed throughout the country (*Encyclopedia of Exhibition,* 1998).

Four Points Drive-in, Tallahassee, Florida. One of thousands of drive-ins that started closing in the late 1970s due to changing viewing habits. (Courtesy of the Florida State Archives)

It was during the 1970s that the country also began to see a host of multiple screens. The practice started in the Midwest when the AMC chain had a theater that was not doing well and decided to put a wall down the middle of it and make two out of it. As simple as it was, this had never been done. Suddenly the theater was doing very well, and the next natural question was: If two works, what about four rooms?

By the early 1970s, theatergoing was no longer offering the evening of spectacle it had for five previous decades. Exhibitors were relying on the economics of multiple screens and a shifting clientele that had become more and more focused toward a younger audience. Allen Michaan, owner of Renaissance Rialto Theatres recalls, "Because of the economy of scale, multiple auditoriums with one staff is unbeatable. When buying movies, you don't know the movie that you are going to play is going to be a good movie or bad movie. It could be a great movie and the public still turns its back on it. So if you have one or two screens, you are stuck with it. If you have fifteen or twenty screens, something will work, ones that work you put into your large auditoriums and things that don't work you put into the small auditoriums" (interview with Allen Michaan, December 2001).

Why did they succeed? The most likely factor is that the public likes them. It is as simple as looking at the convenience factor. One does not have to wait in line to see a movie and mingle with crowds, as the older theater designs required. Audiences can just show up at the local multiplex that is playing the hot new movie on five screens. For theater operators of the multiplex, there was a great economy of scale. They were able to maximize their gross by throwing a movie on a great number of screens during the few weeks it was hot.

This may be convenient for the public, but it came at a great cost for the urban districts of America. The end result was that theatergoers had begun to lose a sense of community that the neighborhood single screen theater had provided. At the same time the theaters began to change, so did the American viewing audience. Older Americans began to attend films less and less. Teens chose their films by what interested them. Action, adventure, monsters and romance were in, but at the expense of further alienating older and younger audience groups.

Chapter 12

The Los Angeles Theater District

No city tells the story of how movies moved from the downtown palaces to the neighborhoods better than Los Angeles. Los Angeles's Broadway entertainment district, located downtown between First and Eighth Streets, houses one of the largest intact collections of movie palaces in the United States. Its growth from 1910 to 1931 tells the history of the glory days of the palace, a story all the more important since the Los Angeles entertainment district was located in the heart of the movie-making capital of the world.

The growth of the theater district did more than create a thriving retail zone; it created a sense of community that extended much further than its eight blocks. By 1931, the year that the last palace was constructed, the street had 12 vaudeville and movie theaters with a combined total of more than 21,500 seats. Before World War II, downtown's Broadway theater district became the central destination for tens of thousands of Angelenos coming from all parts of the city for a busy evening of movies, shopping and eating. The downtown's entertainment districts evolved in two stages beginning in the early 1880s.

ENTERTAINMENT ON MAIN STREET

Downtown Los Angeles in the early 1880s was a relatively small town, with a main street and a residential neighborhood surrounding

Los Angeles Theatre, 1930. Premiere of Charlie Chaplin's *City Lights*. The Los Angeles Theatre, designed by S. Charles Lee, was one of the last great palaces built in the downtown Broadway theater district. (Courtesy of the Theatre Historical Society of America, Elmhurst, Illinois)

it. The original entertainment district centered at first around Child's Opera House in the early 1880s, which eventually evolved into a vaudeville house in the late 1880s going along with the country's vaudeville craze. By the mid-1890s, Thomas Tally opened the city's first penny arcade two blocks south of Child's Opera House. Tally, as mentioned in chapter 2, developed one of the nation's first motion-picture houses. While it was not initially a success, it foretold the national obsession with films that would soon follow.

The commercial district may have started on Main Street, but by the early 1890s, the demands of a quickly growing city pushed the district out further. The commercial district spread out to Spring Street, one block west, and soon to Fort Street, which became known as Broadway by the early 1900s. It was ripe for development since the block had a mixture of small commercial structures that attracted the beginning of an office district (the Bradbury Building at Third and Broadway, 1893) and many lots that still had residential structures.

As Los Angeles began to grow at the turn of the century, retailers looked to the west of Main Street and Spring Street for growth opportunities. Cities like New York had supplied role models of large department stores, and local retailers lost no time in constructing multistoried, steel-reinforced stores that dwarfed the previous commercial outlets or anything seen in the outlying neighborhoods. Up to 1906, the average size of a store was less than 5,000 square feet (Longstreth 1998, p.24). One of the largest retailers in Los Angeles was A. Hamburger and Sons, which had built a four-story dry-goods outlet at Spring Street and Fourth in 1887. Its competition, the Broadway (Broadway and Fourth) built its outlet in 1896.

Within the next decade, these stores would make Broadway their principal home, creating a vibrant retail district. In 1906, a department-store explosion began, with Hamburger and Sons constructing a 500,000-square-foot store at 801 Broadway. It included such features as a steel-reinforced frame wrapped by a classic revival stone surface, an auditorium, doctor and dentist offices, a market, a restaurant and staffed retiring rooms for women customers. Hamburger had also purchased neighboring parcels and helped develop the relatively quiet street into the city's principal shopping district (Longstreth 1998, p.26).

Arthur Letts, owner of the Broadway, soon challenged Hamburger by financing the construction of Bullocks Department Store. John Bullock, a former employee of Letts, created a seven-story structure at Seventh and Broadway that was targeted to an upper-class clientele. It became an overnight success and by 1919 had grown to nearly half a million square feet. Letts enlarged his own store to 460,000 square feet at the same time.

By 1914, the district had begun to suffer from the same problems that Spring Street and Main Street had experienced two decades before: cost and congestion. Broadway had been the home of J.W. Robinson's since 1895. In 1914, it decided to expand, building a 400,000-square-foot store. However, it built at Seventh and Hope, closer to the city's affluent neighborhoods off Figueroa and Adams Street. Competition, lack of parking and land costs began to change the dynamics of retailing.

At the same time that Hamburger and Letts began expanding their stores onto Broadway, exhibition organizations like Pantages realized that the future lay in building larger theaters. Spring Street and Main

Street were already busy, so Pantages too decided to go one block
further to Broadway and built a 1,400-seat film and vaudeville house
at Broadway and Fourth. The theater opened on September 26, 1910.
North of the Pantages, William Clune built a 775-seat theater, Clune's
Broadway, which opened less than two weeks later. Nearby, the
Cameo also opened that year.

This marked the beginning of the Broadway entertainment district,
as several palace-sized theaters were built within five blocks of each
other over the next two decades. By the late 1920s, the district had
well over 20,000 seats, dozens of restaurants and retail establishments
and a rich street vitality unmatched anywhere else in the city. It succeeded in helping create a centralized business district, with finan-
cial institutions located the next block over on Spring Street. Its
success was also, in some ways, a recipe for its demise.

The Broadway of 1900 Los Angeles was similar to New York's
Broadway in name only. As has been described in an earlier chapter,
New York's Broadway was nearly 100 years older, with established
neighborhoods within walking distance of the retail and entertainment districts surrounding Union Square and 14th and 23rd Streets.
New York had built a raised railway system that made this district
accessible to a wide number of people living in the city, and the city
had a denser population than Los Angeles.

Los Angeles in the early part of the twentieth century was growing quickly, but it had a population of only 102,000. Because of the
low cost of land, the Pacific Electric Railroad system was able to
connect the city with nearly 2,000 miles of laid track. The Pacific
Electric even created a downtown terminal and a subway that allowed
access from all parts of the city to Broadway and Spring Streets.

However, Los Angeles was developing along with the automobile.
The population exploded to more than 500,000 by 1920, and the love
affair with cars grew as quickly as the downtown did. This created
a problem that has plagued Los Angeles to this day: automobile congestion. The retail district brought in thousands of shoppers daily.
They competed with office workers and theater patrons for a limited number of parking spaces. For a variety of reasons, city officials
never anticipated the influx of cars and the required parking needs
for their users. Thus one of the primary problems the downtown
faced from 1900 onwards was a lack of coordination between government and business. With no plans for coordinating the location
of parking structures and paying for them, the area suffered a lack
of adequate parking for several decades.

Children's nursery, Los Angeles Theatre, circa 1932. (Courtesy of the Theatre Historical Society of America, Elmhurst, Illinois)

Middle-class shoppers and moviegoers increasingly balked at the lack of parking spaces. The lack of parking spaces in West Coast cities like Los Angeles only hurt the further expansion of the entertainment districts and may have prevented the district from expanding. Longstreth noted that the problems with parking in the downtown retail district helped fan the interest in suburban shopping districts like the Miracle Mile, Hollywood Boulevard and Westwood (1998, p.55). Advertisements for Hollywood and Westwood, two new suburbs, highlighted as one of their main features the fact that their retail outlets had an abundance of parking spaces. They offered both theaters and shopping, with the ease of nearby parking lots.

THE DECLINE OF BROADWAY

Broadway began its initial decline during the early days of the Depression. The area faced several challenges. First, the congestion drove shoppers to regional centers that were developing around the city. The theater industry also faced the combined effects of the Depression and overbuilding. It had overbuilt theaters from coast to coast, and this was especially true on Broadway, where the houses had thousands of seats and high overheads. As audience attendance began to dwindle, theaters faced a challenge in covering their overhead. The Los Angeles Theatre, the last and most luxurious structure built, went bankrupt soon after opening in 1932. The Morosco, which had opened in 1913, changed to an all-newsreel program in 1930.

After World War II, the audience that had come from nearby communities began to choose the comfort of local theaters and drive-ins. However, the Los Angeles downtown movie-palace district survived the loss of its original population by serving the growing minority populations that began to live in the neighborhoods immediately surrounding downtown Los Angeles. Broadway's theaters evolved from serving a primarily white audience to serving an African American population, reflecting changes in the demographics of the nearby neighborhoods in south central Los Angeles during the 1950s and early 1960s. Later the burgeoning Hispanic population moved into the neighborhoods surrounding downtown Los Angeles, and the majority of theaters shifted to playing Spanish-language films. Today, the majority of theaters have been converted to flea markets, jewelry markets, churches and special-event venues such as television production and special film screenings.

The Broadway entertainment district reflects three generations of the community of cinema. It was at one time one of the nation's premier locations for exhibiting films, with its 14 theaters spanning a mile. Later, the street attracted both African American and Hispanic communities to its theaters. Regardless of the audience, the district created a meeting ground that has had the flexibility of finding new communities as old ones move away.

The once-vibrant streets of downtown Los Angeles have become less and less populated during the evenings and weekends. While nighttime on Broadway in New York is very much alive, Los Angeles's Broadway is mostly deserted during the evening hours, a no-man's-land devoid of the masses that had been present only two decades ago.

Where did the audience go? As mentioned earlier, many of the original suburbs like Westwood have become regional centers unto themselves. In later years, the Los Angeles metropolitan district has created a number of entertainment districts that have become primary destinations. These include Citywalk at Universal City, which is a private development mimicking a real-world commercial block that has more than 20 movie screens located at one end. The Santa Monica Promenade has several theater houses located along a walk housing a rich mixture of restaurants and stores. Hollywood Boulevard has Grauman's Chinese Theatre and the El Capitan Theatre surrounded by one of the city's most popular tourist walking districts. Westwood Village has evolved into one of the longest-running entertainment districts in Los Angeles, with several movie houses located within the upscale retail district surrounding UCLA.

City planners in Los Angeles have devised a variety of fixes to revitalize its dying downtown, but there is little literature describing the profound loss of the once-vibrant Broadway entertainment center to the vitality of the urban core. Most planners have not considered theaters an important element of the city or town streetscape. Planners working on the revitalization of downtown Los Angeles concentrated their efforts on creating the Music Center complex, with less then 5,000 total seats. They avoided dealing with the Los Angeles entertainment district that was just five blocks away, a district that featured a variety of immense movie palaces with a total of 25,000 seats that were still being used by inner-city populations during the 1960s but were in imminent danger of closing unless the area's safety, parking and retail mix were reinforced.

Why didn't urban planners and politicians try to save their entertainment districts? Answers may include the fact that the populations using the theaters were not the same ethnic nor economic groups that would use the Music Center. Regardless of the cause, downtown Los Angeles's Broadway entertainment district's infrastructure continued to decline, with little guidance or help from the Los Angeles Downtown Redevelopment Agency, while the Music Center and Opera House structures, located near the newer office towers of Bunker Hill, became the focus of attention.

Chapter 13

Integration: One Town's Story

The movie theater had promised to be a great democratic meeting hall. Films were designed to appeal to the largest audiences, and theaters priced their tickets to make them accessible to the majority of members of the local community. Despite the fact that the movie theater constituted the largest mass-audience meeting hall in modern times, mixing men, women, boys and girls from every religion and social background, it could not counter one social phenomenon that was a fixture of American life in the first six decades of the twentieth century: segregation. Segregationist policies remained locked into American culture well into the 1960s. Segregation was part of the national conscience until the civil rights movement challenged the age-old segregationist policies in place around the country, especially in the southern states.

One of the battlegrounds of the civil rights movement took place in front of the segregated movie theaters that from their earliest days had barred blacks from entering. One of the many towns that fought the battle to integrate was Tallahassee, Florida, the state capital. The town's movie palaces, just down the block from the state capitol building, had a long policy of segregation dating back to their construction in the Depression years, and Tallahassee's first theaters also adhered to the town's Jim Crow statutes.

Picketing the State Theatre in Tallahassee, Florida, 1966. (Courtesy of the Florida State Archives)

Tallahassee is located 18 miles south of the Georgia border and is situated halfway between Jacksonville and Pensacola in the state's northern peninsula. Some refer to this region as the Bible Belt, and its roots go back to a large slavery-based plantation economy that took hold in the first years of the nineteenth century. Tallahassee was founded in 1824 and prides itself on being the only state capital in the South not to have fallen during the Civil War. It has remained a relatively small community, with a 1999 city population of an estimated 125,000.

Regardless of its size and segregationist history, Tallahassee has traversed the same evolution of the growth of entertainment districts that most towns have in America. While segregated theaters may have existed in all parts of the country, nowhere was segregation more de facto than in the Deep South, and Tallahassee is very much considered to be in the Deep South. The town, like similar smaller towns throughout the country, had an entertainment district that began in 1912 and continued to the early 1970s. The story of the town's community of cinema can be broken into several stages.

STAGE ONE: FROM VAUDEVILLE TO THE MOVIES

From 1912 until 1930, the Daffin Theatre, located in the heart of the downtown, serviced the city of 12,500. It was a medium-sized theater, no more than a block from the state legislature, and it was a segregated institution from its first day of business. Before 1920, African Americans were forced to go to the Capital Theatre, started by Mrs. Yellowhair, a graduate of Florida A & M University, the historically black university in Tallahassee. In the early 1920s, African Americans could go to the nearby Leon Theatre located in the historically black "French Town" less than one mile away.

State Theatre, circa 1950. A segregated matinee for the local adolescent white population. (Courtesy of the Florida State Archives)

The Leon Theatre was the only theater African Americans could attend in Tallahassee prior to integration in the 1960s. (Author's collection)

Beginning in 1930, the Daffin found itself competing with the Ritz Theatre on Monroe Street, one block north. Within the next few years, the Ritz Theatre's owner, E.J. Sparks, opened the palace-sized State Theatre across the street on Monroe as well as the Florida Theatre, another movie palace closer to the capitol. These new theaters were located in the heart of the downtown within two blocks of each other as well as the Daffin Theatre. This created a small entertainment district that was surrounded by retail structures, restaurants, civic buildings, the main post office and churches. The community of cinema in Tallahassee, like other areas of its community life, remained segregated.

The Leon Theatre, Tallahassee's colored theater, is remembered as being an attractive and inviting cinema that showed a wide range of films, mostly second run. The biggest complaint among those who remembered going there was the owner censoring the movies to her own moral tastes.

If African American residents of Tallahassee could not find the film they wanted at the Leon, they could drive about 20 minutes northwest to the Leaf Theatre in Quincy, Florida. That theater was built in 1940 with a colored entrance in which residents could avoid white patrons and walk up the stairs to the balcony.

Demonstration in front of the Florida Theater, 1966. The downtown theaters would close soon after they were desegregated. (Courtesy of the Florida State Archives)

STAGE TWO: INTEGRATION

By the mid-1960s, challenges to policies of segregated buses and schools gave hope to local African Americans that change was in the air. James Eaton, director of the Black Archives at Florida A and M University, remembered, "The people tasted freedom, you want more freedom, but you don't get freedom without fighting for it" (interview with James Eaton, December 12, 2000). As historian Anne Roberts, another longtime resident, recalled, "We knew the time had come where we had to get rid of these barriers and the theaters were one of the main targets" (interview with Anne Roberts, December 10, 2000).

The segregated status quo of the entertainment district was directly challenged in a series of emotional demonstrations during civil rights demonstrations of the late 1960s. Eaton recalls the crowds watching the demonstrators "pushing, shoving, spitting and name calling." (interview with James Eaton, December 12, 2000) Town historian Anne Roberts remembered the demonstrations as "awful. Spitting, hostile, yelling and it was so amazing because you would have never believed how people acted" (interview with Anne Roberts, December 10, 2000).

Both the Florida and the State theaters were picketed. After repeated demonstrations, both theaters were desegregated in 1968. Even though the theaters became desegregated, the change was challenging to town residents for the first few years. Anne Roberts remembers that "you were looked at very funny, you were uncomfortable because no one would sit next to you. Very cold. It took a long time to dissipate. It took a long time and when I started taking my kids, I think everybody loves kids, they didn't care what color they were" (interview with Anne Roberts, December 10, 2000).

STAGE THREE: THE ERA OF THE MALL

At the same time that the theaters ended their segregationist policies, Tallahassee's downtown for a variety of reasons lost its entertainment district. The state capital had been able to mix the needs of state government and the local population since 1824, but by the end of the 1960s, the relationship between the state's needs and community shopping and leisure came to an end. Threats were made by state government officials to leave Tallahassee completely for Orlando, and Tallahassee's downtown merchants felt threatened by talk of the state taking over the majority of business locations. A group of merchants decided to build the city's first mall, Northwood, about three miles north of downtown. The mall, including a theater, a Publix market and several retail stores, became the prime regional shopping destination. It was integrated from the first day it was open, with no problems in operations.

Shortly after Northwood opened, a regional mall opened one mile north of the civic center. Tallahassee Mall had large department stores of three chains (Montgomery Ward, Gayfers and Woolco) as hubs, a theater and twice the retail space of Northwood Mall. The opening of these malls had an immediate effect on downtown Tallahassee. Both downtown theaters closed shortly after the Tallahassee Mall's opening. Most downtown retail businesses moved out of the area. Northwood Mall did not survive the regional malls either. Soon after changing the theater into a restaurant in 1974, the mall went into a decline. Never recovering its retail attraction, it rented most of its commercial space to government offices while still retaining its Publix supermarket.

The small but vibrant entertainment district, which at one time had been surrounded by a Sears, numerous cafés, drug stores and other retail outlets, completely disappeared along with its neighboring stores. Both movie palaces became the site of office buildings. Today, Tallahassee's contemporary downtown largely closes up after the government workers leave at 5 P.M. There is little to draw visitors during the evenings or weekends. Ironically, nearly 30 years after the State and Florida theaters left downtown, an IMAX theater is scheduled to open in 2003 one block from the old palaces in an attempt to help once again bring residents back to their downtown.

The contemporary community of cinema is much like any other in the United States. A half dozen multi-screen theaters were built in the suburbs during the 1970s, most adjacent to or part of shopping centers. All but two, both located in large shopping malls, are closed today. In 1988, Rouse Company built Governor's Square, a new regional mall, east of town. Nearby, a multiplex owned by Edwards Cinema and bordering the mall was renovated, offering an eight-screen stadium-style theater. The Tallahassee Mall expanded its theaters, creating an AMC megaplex with stadium seating and art deco motif. The improvement in theater design, including stadium seating, a large entry hall and larger theaters, marks the signs of a new generation of theaters for Tallahassee, nearly 90 years after the first theater came to town.

Part Four

The Return of Spectacle

Chapter 14

Preserving Spectacle

Spectacle is not dead. Across the country, city after city has theaters that have survived the overbuilding of the 1920s, the economic onslaught of the Depression years and the one-two punch of television and the suburban growth movement. In studying how and why they survived, a common theme has emerged: the classic palaces and small-town theaters have become part of the towns' consciousness, one that community members did not want to see disappear. In a larger sense, they are contributing to a much larger social change in how Americans use the urban landscape. Downtowns, whether large or small, are taking on a theme-park quality that encourages residents to take advantage of a wide range of cultural arts, whether classical music, bluegrass, jazz, country, plays or films. It is a movement that has been described as creating an "arts center culture" (Rothstein 1998). Many of the institutions that are housing the arts explosion happen to be the remaining classical theaters. Here are but a few of the survival stories.

THE PARAMOUNT SEATTLE

The Paramount Theatre, designed by famed architect B. Marcus Priteca and opened in 1928, faced a precarious future in the late 1980s. Its ornate décor, one that would be at home in the palace at

Paramount Theatre, Seattle, Washington. The former movie palace is now a thriving regional arts center. (Courtesy of Paramount Theatre, Seattle)

Versailles, was slowly crumbling. More than 70 years of use had faded the once-ornate carpets, the paint and plaster were crumbling, and the entire 3,000-seat theater was covered with layers of dirt and grime on both its interior and exterior.

But the community did not want to let it die. With the leadership of software executive turned theater impresario Ida Cole, the Paramount went through a major transformation into a community arts center. The entire backside of the building was ripped out so the stage could be enlarged to handle contemporary Broadway presentations. Every inch of the theater was restored and cleaned.

The addition solved the existing problem of inadequate backstage facilities. The theater was built for movies and occasional vaudeville performances. It was not prepared for an army of performers and stagehands. Today, several floors are dedicated to dressing and costume rooms. The lead actor's dressing room even features a fireplace and Jacuzzi. The Paramount has become one of the cultural hubs of the Puget Sound community, attracting theatergoers from miles around with a host of Broadway shows, musical talent and classic films.

THE PARAMOUNT IN OAKLAND

Seven hundred miles south of Seattle, in Oakland, California, another Paramount Theatre was originally opened for business in 1931. Designed by San Francisco architect Timothy L. Pflueger, it stands out as one of the preeminent examples of art deco–inspired palace construction. However, it opened just in time for the worst year of the Depression to hit theatrical exhibition. Paramount Publix Corporation went bankrupt, and the theater was eventually sold to the Fox West Coast circuit, but operated as the Paramount until 1970. A changing neighborhood and the expense of maintaining the theater contributed to its closing.

This Paramount, like its cousin in Seattle, also made the transition from deteriorating movie palace to regional arts center. It was initially rescued by the combined efforts of the Oakland Symphony, the city of Oakland and private donors. The Board of Directors of the Oakland Symphony Orchestra Association purchased the building in 1972, and a painstaking restoration was completed in 1973. Restored to its original splendor and fully upgraded to contemporary technical standards, the Paramount now houses productions that represent a wide range of the arts. It is the home of the Oakland Ballet and the Oakland East Bay Symphony. It also hosts a year-round schedule of popular music concerts, variety shows and a classical movie series.

THE ATLANTA FOX

Driving around the streets of downtown Atlanta, it is a memorable experience to come across a movie palace that announces itself on the sidewalk. From a block away, you are aware that you are near a theater unlike any other in the South: the Atlanta Fox.

The Atlanta Fox was originally built in the 1920s as the headquarters for the Shriners' Yaarab Temple Shrine Mosque. It was designed to reflect the grandiose excesses of the 1920s, replete with minarets, onion domes and an ornate exterior only to be outdone by its interior décor. An indoor Arabian courtyard met visitors with a sky flickering with stars and clouds. The immense stage curtains depicted mosques and Moorish rulers in hand-sewn sequins and rhinestones. Every inch of the building, whether it was the entry, the auditorium or telephone booth, was decorated with gilded plaster, bronze and painted detail.

It is not surprising that the high cost of construction would threaten the Shriners' mosque from the outset. The Shriners initially worked out an arrangement with Fox Theatres, which had been expanding its presence in theaters around the country. Without having to go through the ordeal of construction, Fox Theatres found itself with one of the most beautiful palaces in its chain.

As was true for many of the palaces in the country, the Atlanta Fox opened as the Great Depression began, and it went into bankruptcy within two and a half years. The city stepped in and kept it operating, which allowed it to survive the rest of the Depression years. It stayed open and flourished all the way up through the late 1960s.

By the early 1970s, the Fox faced numerous problems. It began to compete with multiplex houses, which were offering a greater variety of films for theatergoers and better terms for movie studios. Much of the Fox's audience had moved to Atlanta's suburbs, and the cost of operating and maintaining the house also increased.

With the threat of a bulldozer looming, the Fox was rescued by a local nonprofit organization, Atlanta Landmarks. After a four-year "Save the Fox" fundraising campaign, the Fox was able to become financially secure. A major renovation program began, with hundreds of local volunteers joining trained professionals in the total restoration of the 4,000-seat house. It soon opened as a regional performing arts center.

In 1987, a second fundraising campaign, "Fix the Fox," successfully raised $4.2 million to improve safety-code compliance and access for the handicapped. Over the years since the restoration began, more than $20 million and hundreds of hours of volunteer time have gone into keeping the Fox open.

What did the community get for its efforts? The Fox has proven itself to be one of the most successful arts centers in the country. Since 1975, it has continuously been able to sustain itself. Nearly every week features a wide variety of activities that are centered in the auditorium or meeting areas, including plays, contemporary and classic films, corporate events, film shoots, weddings and sports presentations.

A special treat is the "Sing-Along" with the "Mighty Moller" organ. "Mighty Mo," a 4,000-pipe theater organ, is maintained, as is the collection of slides of 1930s-era lyrics that are projected to aid patrons in the sing-along. (Atlanta Fox Web site, www.foxtheatre.org/history.htm, February 2002). The Fox has become an integral part of the urban arts movement in Atlanta and helps generate millions of dollars for the local economy through the hundreds of thousands of theatergoers who pass through its doors each year.

NEIGHBORHOOD AND SMALL-TOWN THEATERS

Large urban cities are not the only places that benefit from the renovation of a theater. Neighborhood theaters and small-town theaters have taken on equally important roles in keeping a community's character. For cities across the country, the saving of their theater meant saving their downtown. They realized that the theater represented a lifeblood and needed to be sustained.

In downtown Tunkhannock, Pennsylvania (population 4,400), residents saw their downtown continuously deteriorating since the late 1980s, when the Dietrich, a 1920s-era theater, was closed. With its closing, many of the town's residents realized that the theater represented the heart and soul of the community and began a drive to reopen it. During the late 1990s, the community bought the theater, raising money in a variety of ways, including sponsoring seats for $150 each. The nearby Everhart Museum made the theater a satellite facility, bringing in additional activities to the newly refurbished movie house. Today, the downtown area is once again filled with parked cars, a café has opened, and town residents have a center for gathering once again (Vellela 2001, p.1).

In Quincy, Florida, 20 miles northwest of the state capital, Tallahassee, the Leaf Theatre had been the town's pride and joy ever since it opened in 1940. On opening day, Roy Rogers helped launch a celebration of the state-of-the-art facility, complete with crying room and air conditioning. However, by the 1980s, it had closed, victim of the nearby multiplex offerings in Tallahassee. Community residents, as in Tunkhannock, banded together and decided to reopen it. They had a vision for a regional musical theater, and with the help of a million-dollar restoration grant from a local patron, the Leaf reopened in the mid-1990s as the Leaf Musical Theatre.

A musical theater in the middle of a small town in the Deep South? I had my doubts when I had the opportunity of sitting in the audience during its production of *Fiddler on the Roof*. I can honestly say that it was one of the most enjoyable shows I had seen in years. The performers were all community residents, coming from a hundred-mile radius to perform for their friends and neighbors. Despite sets nearly toppling and the actors' southern accents clashing with their

Leaf Theatre, Quincy, Florida, 2001. (Photo by Arthur Fixel)

attempts at speaking Yiddish, the performance was heartfelt and the audience thoroughly entertained. The Leaf also offers summer performance classes for children in the community and has once again become the life of the Quincy downtown.

Other towns have found that their theater serves as a catalyst for much greater community development than restoring the theater it-

Orinda Theatre, Orinda, California. (Photograph by Tom Paiva. Courtesy of Renaissance Rialto Theaters)

self. That was the case in Orinda, California, minutes away from Oakland and Berkeley, when a developer threatened to tear down the 1941 art deco Orinda Theatre, one of the last classic single-screen theaters built in the San Francisco Bay Area. In the early 1980s, the theater and the surrounding area were purchased by a developer who announced his intention to demolish the theater and surrounding buildings and build a very large retail and office center. There was a loud outcry in the community against his plans, and a number of residents put together a group known as the Friends of Orinda. The initial battle to stop the development fueled greater feelings of powerlessness at being an unincorporated town governed by a county board of supervisors they perceived as unresponsive. The experience caused Orinda residents to organize, incorporate and set up their own city government. The group of area residents ended up fighting the developer all the way to the California Supreme Court and won. The end result was that the theater had to be included in the final design of the center, with a host of restrictions and preservation requirements, costing almost a million dollars in upgrades to the theater alone.

During this process, a local exhibitor with a long history of preserving classic theaters, Allen Michaan, offered to do pro bono work for the group as an industry expert. On a number of occasions he had gone to public hearings and talked about the value of the theater. Though he was on the opposing side during the fight, the development company decided that Michaan was the best tenant that it could get and ended up awarding his company, Renaissance Rialto, the management of the theater.

The Orinda has turned out to be a successful theater for Renaissance Rialto. The theater is surrounded by an open-air shopping mall with restaurants and stores. Michaan feels that the best thing about the Orinda theater is its three-story underground parking garage. "That is what makes the theater viable and that helps the theater tremendously. It goes back to parking. Aside from it being so beautiful, that goes back to one of the root causes for why it is such a popular theater. We've got parking" (interview with Allen Michaan, December 2001).

KEEPING THE PALACES ALIVE

Among Michaan's theaters is one of the few remaining movie palaces in the Bay Area that exclusively shows films: the Grand Lake Theatre. "It was developed by a couple of local theater entrepreneurs, Karski and Italiski," Michaan recalls, "and they built a number of theaters in the Bay Area. Pretty big grandiose theaters. At the time it was built in 1926 it was for a brief period of time the largest theater west of the Mississippi" (interview with Allen Michaan, December 2001).

That designation did not last long. During the late 1920s, people were building palaces everywhere, and the Grand Lake's 2,200 seats were soon overtaken by other theaters in Los Angeles and San Francisco. However, it was very expensive in its day, costing almost a million dollars, it was a very deluxe theater, and in 1928 it became part of the West Coast Fox Theatre circuit. It remained in the Fox West Coast Group until it became a National General theater in the 1950s, and in the early 1970s it was sold to Mann Theatres. In 1979, Michaan bought the Grand Lake from Mann Theatres.

Michaan faced a major problem with the Grand Lake. The single-screen theater had well over 2,000 seats. With the multiplex phenomenon setting the standard for theaters, he realized that he had to add

Grand Lake Theater, Oakland, California. (Photograph by Tom Paiva. Courtesy of Renaissance Rialto Theaters)

screens to the house for it to survive. Michaan explained that "these types of buildings naturally attracted me, but the survival rate for theaters like Grand Lake and my other theaters is abysmal because they cannot compete with the megaplex" (interview with Allen Michaan, December 2001).

Michaan decided to divide the theater up. He left the main screen, complete with the organ, downstairs. The balcony became the second screen in 1981. In 1985, two others were added on the side in the former storefront retail space. "It's a very grandiose theater and in dividing it and expanding it we tried to be very sensitive and respectful to the décor and to all the changes and improvements that were made here. We have tried to hold true to the whole idea of fantasy and opulence" (interview with Allen Michaan, December 2001).

Michaan's background prepared him for the task of making the Grand Lake a success. He began showing films in the early 1970s in Berkeley, renting auditoriums in and around campus. He remembers, "In 1972 I opened the Rialto Theatre in a warehouse on Gilman Street which was built out of salvaged materials from theaters that were being torn down. It was a counterculture type of cinema" (interview with Allen Michaan, December 2001). What Michaan discovered was that the cinema not only entertained, but spoke to various communities in the city.

In the early 1970s, his theater became a gathering spot for adherents of the counterculture, who helped define their own feelings about politics and society with anti-Nixon festivals, anti-Reagan festivals and *Reefer Madness* screenings. "The Rialto became a real counterculture icon. And it became very popular and successful. I started from there, I started acquiring and restoring and operating old movie theaters" (interview with Allen Michaan, December 2001).

Today the Grand Lake is the center of the Piedmont/Lakeshore shopping district, a landmark structure located in the heart of a thriving commercial district. Michaan feels that the theater is succeeding despite the lack of parking immediate to the property. "My theaters seem to hang on pretty decently because they are so grand and so wonderful and so beautiful that enough people still are going out of their way to come here to see a movie and choose a Grand Lake over a megaplex to see a film they want to see" (interview with Allen Michaan, December 2001).

The original décor of the theater's auditorium can be best described as classical Greco-Roman with a lobby that is French Renaissance. When Michaan added the third and fourth theaters in 1985, these two auditoriums were built in what was previously storefront rental property. "They were retail space that was part of the original building. In the 1920s when theaters of this size were built, they normally were built with retail stores attached because it was the norm that any retail space that was immediately contiguous to the theater was the best retail space in that district because that is where the action is. In those days, you would have a candy shop and soda fountain because you didn't have a snack bar in theaters in the 20s" (interview with Allen Michaan, December 2001). It was not until the 1940s, when film companies started charging exhibitors more for film rentals, that exhibitors decided to find other forms of income, and concessions turned out to be the best way. "We took the four or five units that were there and gutted that part of the building and created 2 auditoriums, one in an Egyptian motif and one in a Moorish motif. And actually at the time I built those theaters in 1985, those were the first movie palaces that were built in the United States since the 1940s. It was sort of that I was reviving an art form that had been lost for 40 years" (interview with Allen Michaan, December 2001).

LIVING WITH THE MEGAPLEX

The Grand Lake is very much a unique institution. For the most part, movie palaces that show films are a rare breed in the twenty-first century. Michaan points out that lack of parking is hurting most urban theaters, despite their convenient proximity to neighborhoods. "Location is wonderful, but parking is not as easy as if you are in the middle of a shopping center and for a lot of people that becomes a deciding factor unfortunately. People are lazy to a point where [they say] 'I don't want to go to the Grand Lake because I will have to drive around for five minutes and walk a block,' as opposed to going to a theater with a parking structure right next door to it or acres of free parking all around it. A lot of people opt for the easier parking environment and it costs us a lot of customers" (interview with Allen Michaan, December 2001).

Today's audiences have accepted the megaplex theaters and for the most part prefer them. Downtown theaters, especially if they have a single screen or if they have added two, three or four screens, have found it difficult to survive. Michaan points out that the effect this has on the communities both downtown and in neighborhood theaters can be very destructive. "As theaters go away, it has a domino effect on the rest of the businesses around it. Especially anything that counts on nighttime entertainment like restaurants. They are the first to go. And it's a bad process, damaging process, affecting the whole fabric of the country" (interview with Allen Michaan, December 2001).

The growth in megaplex-style theaters is not the only problem facing the classic single-screen theater. Both face another common threat that is looming in America's not-too-distant future. Over the movie theater's hundred-year history, it has faced a number of challenges. In the late 1920s, there was a complete economic meltdown of the economic system of the country that caused the Great Depression. During the 1950s, television cut into the audience. However, today, an entirely new set of problems faces theater exhibition.

The big theater companies have overbuilt and are overinvested. They are vulnerable to a tremendous shock if there is a slight downtick in the number of people who are buying tickets to the movies. It may not be the economy, however, that hurts the theater industry today, but the growing use of home entertainment centers. Allen Michaan's biggest worry is people staying home and appreciating the home theater better than the big screen. "I am very much in the minority in the industry but I personally believe we are just now seeing a whole entertainment revolution that is going to devastate the theaters today much in the same way that television did to theaters in the early 1950s. Right now we have the very beginnings of high-definition TV. It is a very expensive product and there still is not a lot of product that you can bring in on hi-def TV. But by law FCC has mandated that broadcasts must go out on both analog and hi def by 2005 and at the same time we are seeing the very beginning of and quick acceleration of technology in plasma screens—flat screens —and what I think we will see happen in short order over the next few years is high definition. You will see the availability of big screens, plasma monitors and the prices are going to plummet as people begin buying them in mass just like what happened to VCRs" (interview with Allen Michaan, December 2001).

His fear has historical merit. Twenty years ago the first video-cassette recorder, the Sony Betamax, cost more than $2,000. The tapes were $15–$20 an hour for the raw tape, and there was very little product available to screen. Twenty years later, the cost of the VCR has come down to less than $100, tapes cost as little as a dollar, and thousands of titles are available. It is not difficult to imagine the same thing happening to the plasma television products.

Classic theaters with limited screens are also facing challenges from other areas. They have to contend with ever-increasing costs of energy, payroll and insurance. Insurance costs in particular have sky-rocketed throughout the theater exhibition market, especially since the September 11, 2001, terrorist attacks.

Michaan believes that the theater will survive, but in a much more limited role. "Twenty years from now, there will be a handful of very elite special places like the Grand Lake that survive, or maybe the strongest and the biggest and the most intensely built up megaplexes that survive, while the other megaplexes fall by the wayside. In the East Bay [region of the San Francisco Bay Area], where now we have 25 megaplexes, maybe there will be 5 that will be in business. I don't see how the home video revolution cannot have a terrible impact on the theater exhibition industry. We keep getting new types of technology and new types of hardware like DVDs. So far we don't have hi-def DVD, but in a few years we will. People are getting more cognizant of quality. So now you can have a clearer sharper brighter image in your home TV than any theater with better sound and more comfortable seats than any commercial theater can hope to offer" (interview with Allen Michaan, December 2001).

Michaan is fearful that the further loss of theaters will have a negative effect on urban community life. "I would call it a keystone or foundation and the theater is the magnet that brings in the people and the economic activity that comes along with them. That is what powers and fuels the downtown business district. And as that portion goes away, everyone else suffers. Some businesses suffer, some businesses go under, but everyone is hurt. I think it creates a sense of community. The value is basically being something where you have a core business district where they congregate and they feel comfortable at night. Because they are not alone. Because they have a place to go out and walk around and mingle and go into restaurants and window shop and whatever, it's fun for people. It draws them out of their homes. All too often we go to our homes. We close our doors, barricade ourselves in and it's too much cocooning. It's a good social phenomenon to be around a bunch of people instead of being isolated. And there is cultural value to see a comedy in a room full of people that are also laughing. It makes it more fun. There are a lot of pluses for that" (interview with Allen Michaan, December 2001).

Chapter 15

The Megaplex and Beyond

In 1928, near Fifth and Broadway in downtown Los Angeles, a somewhat unusual retail structure was built: the Arcade Building. The multistory building included an indoor shopping mall, inspired by arcade structures that had been built in England and towns in the United States such as Providence, Rhode Island, and Cleveland, Ohio. It had shops and restaurants, similar to the older arcades. However, it structurally added something different: a movie theater and vaudeville house. Little did the architects and builders realize that they had built one of the earliest prototypes of what we have come to know as the mall, the structure that has played such an important part in changing the nature of Main Street and America's central business districts.

The Arcade Building's combination of retail establishments and restaurants with a theater now exists as the ubiquitous mall in all reaches of the United States. From 1995 to 1997, 21,269 movie screens were built, the great majority of which were located within the confines of an enclosed shopping mall (*Encyclopedia of Exhibition* 1998). Malls have become the new entertainment districts, climatically controlled and privately patrolled.

The pedestrian mall's relationship with the theater goes back to the earliest malls designed by Victor Gruen and Associates. In 1948, Northgate Mall, the first regional mall in the United States, opened in north Seattle. The mix of commercial structures was not unlike that of most commercial main streets. A large department store served as the anchor (Seattle's Bon Marche) and occupied nearly a quarter of the 800,000 square feet. The rest of the mall was composed of 80 tenants, whose stores guaranteed competitive merchandising.

The primary design features of the pedestrian mall that set it apart from the downtown were its private space and that it aimed at limiting the distance between stores and parking. It served as the prototype mall structure, with outside parking and a controlled inside walking corridor. The mall had a medical and professional building built at its northern end and a large theater in back of it.

In the years after the Northgate Mall was built, theaters throughout the United States lost their original goal of spectacle. Multiplex construction was often tied to malls or located near malls, but was minimalist in design and attraction.

THE CONTEMPORARY MALL

No form of architecture describes contemporary society as does the mall. It has, according to mall architect Jon Jerde, become its own Main Street, a destination unto itself. Jerde notes that "Americans, unlike Europeans, do not stroll aimlessly, but in fact need a destination, a sense of arrival at a definite location." This was his goal in designing both San Diego's Horton Plaza and Los Angeles's Westside Pavillion, which in his words provided "destinations that are also a public parade and a communal center"(Forsher and Banerjee 1995).

Ann Friedberg has described the contemporary nature of the mall as a "consumer theme park" in which one "strolls through a phantasmagoric array of commodified images and experiences." The combination of the multiplex cinema and the shopping mall is one that sells "the pleasures of imaginary mobility as psychic transformation" (1993, p.xi). These spaces, which allow public access, are not the same as public spaces that we would find on the streets. Like the arcade before, they offer a sense of safety, refuge from foul weather and the convenience of shopping and parking in the same location.

Today, spectacle has returned, and with a vengeance. This vision of life, which is more reminiscent of a scene from a film, ties in with the theme-park consumer experience. As movies take us to another realm, so does the theme-park mall. These shopping malls have become a metaphorical extension of the "place" created by the community of cinema. The central business district has been changed in many ways. Old commercial and entertainment districts have moved into the malls. Museums, public-domain plazas, civic buildings, broad avenues and civic sculptures have become the exception.

As different as malls may be from Main Street, it can also be argued that they still have more to share with their distant cousin than not. The theme park/mall is a world of various commercial enterprises, just as was the entertainment district of the 1920s. The mingling in public spaces may now occur in private spaces in today's theme parks/malls, but private spaces were also the mingling ground in the 1920s, when thousands would find themselves face-to-face inside massive department stores and movie palaces. The theme parks/malls' architecture borrows from a multitude of design features, also a mark of entertainment-district design.

In the early 1980s, architects and builders began to realize that spectacle—the vital part of exhibition—had disappeared both in quality and quantity. The theaters' link to the neighborhood, offering an unusual environment that amused theatergoers, had been replaced by boxes with curtains that became the norm in minimalist-inspired multiplex theaters that dotted the country starting in the late 1960s.

New theater designs began to draw on motifs from the classical and art deco designs that defined the old inner-city movie-palace districts. Weekly attendance went from a low of 17 million in 1972 to more than 23 million by 1985. The number of theaters and screens also increased, going from 11,670 in 1972 to 21,097 in 1985. Profits also increased as revenues from ticket sales grew from $1,583,000,000 in 1972 to $6,365,000,000 in 1997 (*Encyclopedia of Exhibition* 1998, p.232). Today's megaplex theater in a mall is in many ways reminiscent of the entertainment district of the 1920s, with a similar economic core and a visual presentation that makes the theater experience—to paraphrase Marcus Loew's comment from nearly 70 years ago—as interesting as the films themselves.

WHAT NEXT? MALLS, THEATERS AND THE CONTEMPORARY AUDIENCE

The contemporary theater owner has a much different set of concerns than exhibitors faced just one decade ago. Among the problems facing today's theater is the link between films and violence in society. With the societal concern about violence and safety, exhibitors have worked hard through the National Association of Theatre Owners (NATO) to alleviate problems at the box office. President

Bill Clinton, shortly before leaving office, highlighted the problems and the attempted solutions in an address to theater owners, reminding them that "the great thing about the multiplex is that there's a movie for every member of the family, but not every movie is for every member of the family. When you drop them off, you shouldn't have to worry about your G-rated kids getting into violent or suggestive R-rated movies. Too often children do get past the ticket counter, unescorted and under-age. I'm pleased to announce today the theater owners are clearly drawing the line. The nation's largest group of theater owners has agreed to ask young people for IDs at R-rated movies. From now on, parents will know that the R-rating means what it is supposed to mean—restricted, no one under 17 without a parent or guardian" (White House speech, June 8, 1999).

In addition to social concerns that affect both the mall and the movie theater, the contemporary cinema experience in the mall is changing with the growth of a new generation of megaplex theaters. One company that is paving the way for a redefinition of the contemporary moviegoing experience is Muvico Theaters, based in Fort Lauderdale, Florida. The rapidly growing company operates a number of motion-picture theaters around the southeastern United States, but its theaters are unlike most conventional megaplexes in several important ways.

Muvico president Hamid Hashemi has been in theatrical exhibition for nearly 20 years. Before undertaking his vision of the future theater, he wanted to understand who constitutes the contemporary audience as well as get a better understanding of why nontheatergoers were staying away. "I did a study on trying to understand what made theaters successful. Looking at the theaters that were built in the 1920s and 1930s, when theaters were experiencing their highest attendance, we realized that besides the movies themselves, the theaters created the sense of escapism with their detailed atmospheric designs, therefore enhancing the movie-going experience. Walking into a theater was like walking into a different world" (interview with Hamid Hashemi, October 2001). In the study his company conducted in the late 1990s, the research pointed to a number of important findings about today's motion-picture audience. Among the results were the following:

- The most common leisure activity among adults was going out to dinner, with an average of 42 visits over a 12-month period.

Watching videos or going out to listen to live music was second, with 20 visits a year. Going to movies was fifth, with an average of 8 trips a year. Compare this to the 1920s and 1930s, when nearly half of American families went weekly to the theater.

- Teens were the most active moviegoers, with 17 visits in a period of a year. Again, compared to studies of audiences in the 1920s and 1930s with teen attendance in the 60 percent weekly range, the audience had shrunk considerably, but was nevertheless still active.

- One out of three adults surveyed went to the theaters at least once a month, with the adult audience being 18–34-year-olds. Groups most likely not to go to theaters were adults over 45 as well as adults with lower income levels. Adults who took advantage of other leisure activities and/or were of a higher income level (above $35,000 annually) were more likely to be moviegoers also.

- The majority of teens are frequent moviegoers. Nearly one-third of teens aged 16 to 18 go to between 13 and 25 films a year. A surprising finding was that 11 percent of preteens (aged 12 to15) reported seeing more than 100 films a year. In all, 75 percent of teens are frequent moviegoers (at least one movie a month), and 20 percent of teens are superfrequent moviegoers, going four or more times a month to the theaters. Ethnic teens and preteens from all groups turned out to be superfrequent moviegoers also. Teen attendance was not tied to household income.

Hashemi realized that a number of changes had to be made to the design and function of the theater if he was going to attract a larger audience. One of the first things he did was to sell off his older generation of theaters. "I sold all my old theaters in 1995 before the megaplex trend started. I didn't want to be saddled with obsolete theaters" (interview with Hamid Hashemi, October 2001). He saw that the economics and social conditions that had made his older theaters successful in the past would not match his ambitious plans for the future megaplex.

The new Muvico megaplex promised to indulge "its guests with a total entertainment experience from the moment they arrive, bringing back the 'big event' experience enjoyed by the guests of the great movie palaces of the 20's and 30's" (Muvico public relations announcement 1999). Hashemi and his architects studied more than

1,500 movie palaces from the 1920s and 1930s, picking out architectural features that would provide a feeling of spectacle for audiences from the moment they arrived. The architects and designers of these theaters decided that the feeling of grandeur had to "be every step of the way. All the way including the interior bathroom. Every element must be themed" (Muvico public relations announcement 1999).

Among the physical signatures of the Muvico chain are a porte cochere with valet parking. The Davie, Florida, Muvico Paradise 24 Theatre offers an impressive classical Egyptian-style porte cochere that greets guests as they arrive. "The grand entryway offers a sense of arrival to a big event," Mr. Hashemi noted. "On a typical Friday, the valet will park 800 cars and on a Saturday, over 1,200 cars" (interview with Hamid Hashemi, October 2001).

The modern Muvico megaplex theaters have attempted to create the experience of spectacle by providing imposing entry facades, hand-painted soaring atriums and domed rotunda lobbies. The physical grandeur has been complemented by the latest in technological improvements. Just as the first palaces impressed audiences with the new technologies of air conditioning and films with sound, the Muvico megaplex has incorporated state-of-the-art Dolby digital surround sound, wall-to-wall curved screens and movable chairs.

Entrance to Muvico Egyptian 24, Hanover, Maryland. The contemporary theaters feature the spectacle-driven environment of the old movie palaces with modern comforts. (Courtesy, Muvico Theaters)

Muvico Paradise 24, Davie, Florida. The interior entry area is reminiscent of movie palaces of the 1920s and 1930s. (Courtesy, Muvico Theaters)

Hashemi also realized that along with spectacle and technology, one had to promise good service. "We have been focused on good service. We have been growing slowly. We are always concerned with how to better the experience" (interview with Hamid Hashemi, October 2001).

Another unique quality of the Muvico palaces is the inclusion of restaurants. Muvico's research had shown that nearly 85 percent of audiences eat before they see a film. Young professionals who are typically not married often go out to restaurants but limit the theater to special occasions. Muvico came up with a solution, full-service restaurants in the theater, common in the 1920s, but unheard of in the last four decades of the twentieth century. "We have changed that pattern for many people. We offer a balcony, a bar and two restaurants with private entrances that cater to the young professional and those on a date looking for an intimate experience while still enjoying the full effect of the big screen presentation" (interview with Hamid Hashemi, October 2001).

Muvico child care center. (Courtesy, Muvico Theaters)

Hashemi sees the megaplex of the future in a much different way than a theater that simply is located within a mall. He envisions the megaplex as a gathering place, more like a church, that should be an institution unto itself. "Our theaters are living beside the mall. The mall is not going away. Shoppers kill time by combining entertainment and shopping. Now, and in the future, I see a shift toward the theater" (interview with Hamid Hashemi, October 2001).

Another group that Muvico focuses on attracting is families. As the price of childcare has increased over the years, many families have been priced out of going to the movie theater. The theater with childcare is almost unheard of today. Back in the 1920s and the 1930s, it was not uncommon for large theaters to have crying rooms where parents could take their children and not miss any of the film. Hashemi wanted to bring that inclusiveness back with modern sensibilities. He also wanted to get young families back, and childcare was the solution. Mirroring the idea of childcare that Samuel "Roxy" Rothapfel had introduced in the Alhambra Theatre eight decades earlier, Hashemi introduced a child-friendly theater. The "children's playroom" is a facility designed for children between the ages of three and eight, where parents can drop their children off and enjoy a movie. "It's one of the most successful ventures we have ever done. We have regular people come on a weekly basis. We have safety procedures similar to a hospital. And we charge $10 for 3 hours" (interview with Hamid Hashemi, October 2001).

Hashemi has attempted to redefine the contemporary megaplex experience, combining the best of modern technology with the spectacle of the movie palaces' golden age. He has subscribed to the idea immortalized in the quote often attributed to movie producer Samuel Goldwyn, "There is first class and there is no class." As Hashemi prefers to say, "Other groups have tried to do this but shortchanged the public. If you do it, do it the right way!" (interview with Hamid Hashemi, October 2001).

Chapter 16

Cinema and the City

The theater has served as a public gathering space, adjusting to the wishes of the community and the changes in technology. Over its hundred-year history, the public space that the theater creates has evolved from vaudeville shows to palaces, multiplexes and now the privacy of high technology home theaters. The audience is still out there; the main element that has changed today is the location of the screen.

Entertainment districts, which served as the home to theaters for over a century, have continuously been evolving, largely due to the effects of information and communication technologies. These technologies, which have been examined in earlier chapters, have shaped the structure of society with the introduction of motion pictures. The motion picture also changed the social patterns of cities, going back to the first nickelodeons, with institutions such as churches suffering dramatic decreases in attendance as early as the turn of the century when audiences shifted their attendance to the theater (Lynd and Lynd 1929).

In the central business district of yesteryear, certain elements came to symbolize Main Street structures. Symbols included the tall church spires, a town-hall cupola, carved and molded bank doors, the jeweler's clock and the cigar-store Indian. With the introduction of new activities downtown after 1900, other icons began to be generated, including

Audience going to Nickel Theater, circa 1910. (Courtesy of the Florida State Archives)

soda-fountain Coca-Cola signs, the movie marquee and the gas station's logo. All of these have become elements in developing contemporary themes for malls, creating an immediate but artificial sense of history despite the lack of a history.

In the midst of this spectacle-driven public space sits the movie theater. Its physical space has become part of the evolving use and understanding of the ways that time and space interact with both our urban form and social structure. The paradigm shifts described by Manuel Castells (1996; Castells and Hall 1994) and other writers over the years have used terms that include both "city" and "society" in portraying the environment of the change. One challenge researchers face with the current paradigm shifts is understanding and acknowledging exactly the environment in which this shift is happening. Is it in fact the urban space? Is it the social organization, or is it an evolving combination of both? Social organizations work in a physical space and have a complex relationship with that space, but they are not that space.

EFFECTS OF INFORMATION AND COMMUNICATION TECHNOLOGIES ON DISCUSSION OF PLACE

It is becoming increasingly easier for social activities to avoid taking place in a public space, let alone even a physical environment. Michael Davis has called for a crusade to "secure the city against the destruction of any truly democratic urban space" (1992, p.155). The city that Davis fears is one that has turned inward for protection, one in which urban space has been supplanted by "electronic space" and the mall has supplanted the traditional Main Street.

Michael Sorkin (1992) has gone so far as to suggest that phones and modems have killed the streets. However, for some writers on contemporary urban environments, the modern-day electronic meeting areas are not public places. They are, as Edward Soja has described them, "noncityness" (1992, p.94). The public use of place, in other words, may be disappearing, and the movie theater may be one of the principal casualties.

The argument of a decline in the urban realm, made by such authors as Robert E. Putnam (1995) and Sorkin (1992), implies that at one time we had a downtown sense of place that offered us a greater opportunity for "connectiveness." It can, however, be argued that this may be a shortsighted perspective. If we choose to see "place" as a location for gathering, the definition has always implicated the problems of inclusion and exclusion. The Greek agora, for example, may at first glance be considered an early model of democratic gatherance, but in reality it excluded both slaves and women, the majority of the local population. In the last 100 years, many cities in the United States featured streets where all citizens could converge. On a closer look, however, we can point to nineteenth-century commercial districts that barred unchaperoned women from walking down commercial streets for fear that they might be pointed out as prostitutes. The streets these women could not walk were also the locations of clubs and saloons that were segregated by class and race as well as hotels that often were "restricted." Southern towns may have had an air of gentility, but they limited access of African Americans to drinking fountains, restrooms, buses, theaters and restaurants. Broad streets, plazas and marketplaces may have encouraged intermingling, but by no means did they offer an environment that could truly be called democratic and nonexclusive.

If we reconsider and allow our definition of place and space to be more flexible, as realms that are being continuously redefined, we may start to reinterpret the modern-day meeting grounds as examples of a new paradigm. "Place" has been often characterized by a physical dimension, but because of advances in information technologies, a new type of urban place has evolved which Melvin Webber has described as a "non-place urban realm" (1964).

During the twentieth century, cities have increasingly utilized information and communication technologies in developing their infrastructure operations, but the reliance on information technologies is much greater today than ever before. Information technology systems have continued to develop, especially with the aid of the computer, in such a way as to define the postmodern city as an "intelligent city."

David Harvey suggests that as the walls of distance fall, "we become more sensitized to what the world's spaces contain" (1989, p.294). The importance of space, coupled with the increase in imagery, has created a new understanding of our environment. The focus on spaces in a world saturated with images has had a profound effect on the design of commercial spaces for public uses.

INFORMATION AND COMMUNICATION TECHNOLOGIES AND PHYSICAL SPACE: DECLINE OR TRANSFORMATION?

Information technologies have had dramatic effects on the development of the central urban district. One has to look back no further than the 1880s, when the telephone's introduction changed the physical design of the downtown by allowing the practical use of skyscrapers (Pool 1977). Two decades later, motion pictures, through their exhibition in theaters, helped create a new sense of place, examined in chapters 1 through 4, that has been described as a "community of the cinema." Information technologies have not so much "destroyed" physical space as they have contributed to increasing the variety of new types of places and, in so doing, have made it much harder to define and delimit these spaces. Jeff Weintraub points out that the key to understanding the concept of "public" has less to do with the state, obligations and solidarity and more to do with sociability (1995, p.284).

The contemporary nonplace realm has created a hybrid composite of privately owned but publicly used interior spaces found in malls, airport terminals, atrium lobbies of hotels, convention centers and office buildings. Another form of nonplace realm is the "public quasi-space" of e-mail and the Internet.

It has been noted that urban environments in the past helped develop and nurture a sense of community by the construction of parks, walking streets and plazas. Over the past century, the contemporary city, as Michael Sorkin has pointed out, has evolved to become a "conceptual space." He notes that what is missing today "is not a matter of a particular building, but the space between the connections that make sense of the form" (1992, p.xii).

Richard Sennett theorized that when the city deteriorated and lost its vitality, the role of the family expanded. Sennett describes the public sector of the nineteenth century as collapsing in the postindustrial age and people reacting as if they could fill the void by extending the private family sector. Today, "We are witnessing the inability of the family to fulfill all the many functions with which it has been invested, no doubt temporarily, during the past half century" (1977, pp.234–235).

It has been argued that modern technologies are among the causes of the "breakdown" of our community culture. Putnam (1995) points to the amount of time that Americans spend watching television, taking their attention away from the communities that the author believes are more socially connective. Putnam's argument, while often grounded in empirical data, goes to his gut-level feelings when he assesses the true costs of communication technologies. While his perspectives are more polemic than systematic research, they nevertheless represent a concern that has become commonplace in the social science community.

The influence of information technologies on the infrastructure is a relationship that can best be described as interactive, interdependent and complementary. This can be seen in such relationships as the coordination of traffic by an electronically guided lighting system, the governing of rail transport by radio and location-seeking devices or the satellite-aided locating technology.

Will the growing use of information technologies create a society that destroys our ability to separate public from private space? We are already living in a world in which activities are watched in every bank, mall and convenience store and on a growing number of street corners by cameras hooked up to police monitoring stations. We are living in a world where privacy is becoming a rare commodity.

The price paid for keeping our previously developed assumptions of public and private space may not be affordable over time. The changes in technology and subsequent use of the new tools that are introduced suggest some difficult questions. Will we give up our democratic freedoms for an increased feeling of security? How will the commodification of our commercial world be controlled? As electronic space becomes increasingly owned by private sources, who will gain access without fees (Openshaw and Goddard, 1987)?

Another challenging issue revolves around losing our "sense of freedom" as managers utilize information technologies as a means for creating what Michel Foucault (1979) refers to as a "disciplinary society." Will the various incarnations of information technologies create a modern-day version of Jeremy Bentham's "panopticon," the device that would establish an environment in which the inmate or worker could be observed continuously?

The urban infrastructure in major Western cities face a crisis today, a crisis that includes antiquated delivery and access systems whose rehabilitation and renewal will be expensive because they were built for levels of use far below the current and projected demands on them. In addition to these problems, the infrastructure is challenged by the growing demands of transporting goods and people through urban areas. Information technologies have been implemented with the goal of helping reduce the demands on the infrastructure, for example, use of electronic aids in tollbooths, freeway regulation and air corridor control.

Information technologies can also be credited, on the other hand, with increasing demands on the infrastructure. The growth of the use of mobile phones, for example, has allowed a greater freedom from the place of employment and out onto the streets, increasing the density of congestion on the roads—not to mention inattentive drivers.

Information technologies have also played a role in issues relating to access to the public space. As the "gatekeepers" of information take greater and greater control of cultural content, another factor affecting society is the capability to receive the information. As it was common for the poor at the turn of the twentieth century to be excluded from telephone service (Pool 1977), so too the revolution of information technologies may limit itself to the upper-income strata of society. This projects a future in which we further impoverish areas that were already economically challenged.

Over the past three decades, the concept of a "neighborhood" where community and culture meet on the street (Jacobs 1962) has now evolved to include electronic neighborhoods that create "new ways of clustering."

What does this mean for the cinema and the city? Potential scenarios for the future city range from large cities that will continue to grow to a move toward smaller cities that will offer cheaper jobs, cheaper lifestyles and different roles in the economic fulfillment of the corporation of the twenty-first century. Either model will mean a future of increased displacement for those who do not fit into the remolding of the job market.

The community of cinema stands at the forefront of defining community today, and as such it is an indicator of what public space has evolved into. Do the changes in our society add up to a decline in our use and appreciation of public space? Are we making an argument that the past should be our standard to uphold? If so, many in our culture would not agree, since for many a return to the public realm of the past means a repressive, controlled society in which exclusion was more common than today. We need to begin to examine what elements of the past are worth holding onto and how one can integrate these into a continuously changing urban realm that places less and less importance on time, space and distance as deciding factors in how we share our "public space."

Conclusions

Over the past 16 chapters, the history and culture of the movie theater have been defined by the relationship between the theater, public space, retail districts and community. It would be presumptuous to conclude that the movie theater has been the major factor in the decay of downtown. It was a player, but so were changes in neighborhood economies, traffic patterns, industrial flight and a host of other factors. It would also be presumptuous to assume that the movie theater was the primary factor in introducing spectacle to our culture as a normative event. This would preclude the involvement of the actual films shown in theaters, television, the print media, amusement parks, and the general movement to create "invented-street" regional malls.

It is not presumptuous, however, to conclude that the movie theater has been a major player in all these areas. The community of cinema has been in many ways a barometer of the evolution of place over the past century. City planners and urban historians, however, have spent a century putting on rose-colored glasses in evaluating the history of the downtown in America, focusing on what they wanted to see and avoiding the movie theater as relatively unimportant to the story. However, the evolution in America's entertainment districts cannot be told by focusing just on capitalist expansion or social alienation. It is a story that began with the movie theater and has evolved

Actress Gloria Stuart (right) entering the Roxy, 1946. (Reproduced from the Collections of the Library of Congress)

into a much broader community that has moved into malls, restored downtowns and home theaters as it continually redefines itself.

This book has explored how the growth and decline of the inner city was not limited to workers going to and from their jobs. It was not just shoppers coming downtown to get their clothes. It also included—at its height—over half the country's population going weekly to the downtown or neighborhood commercial district and commingling, eating together, watching a movie together and sharing an experience on a scale that had never been equaled.

In the past, the community of cinema existed in the central business district. It was a huge community and could be found in almost every city across the United States. These were communities that shared dreams, entertainment, shopping, meals and friendships. The theater became the environment for shared fantasies, and it became a meeting ground for the masses. With nearly five generations having shared the experience, the theaters have become part of our shared national heritage.

Palaces may no longer be practical for movie exhibition, but they have provided new homes for performing arts centers and retail outlets. Whether in Seattle, Washington, Oakland, California, or Syracuse, New York, the old Paramount and Fox theaters live on, using spectacle to supply the environment for live stage productions. The live stage houses of 1900 New York inspired these palaces, and they once again serve that purpose.

Today, the community of the cinema may be different, but it is still very much alive. While the number of theater sites is less than a third of what it was in 1930, the number of screens has increased to more than 31,050, 6,000 more than existed at the height of the movie palaces (*Encyclopedia of Exhibition* 1998). Today, they are seldom in the downtown entertainment district, which has largely disappeared. Typically they are located in the new commercial districts, most often in or near a mall, and they are attempting once again to offer the same spectacle that the theater offered five decades before. The number of participants may not be the same compared to the total populations that attended years ago; the age of the audience may be younger; and the palaces of 3,000 seats are now theaters of less than 1,000. However, the experience of sharing a movie with a group is still the same, and the historic lessons of retail tie-ins, central locations and an environment that attracts people have not changed.

MOTION PICTURE THEATER AND THE GROWTH OF THE CENTRAL BUSINESS DISTRICT AND URBAN NEIGHBORHOODS

The movies became an integral part of the experience of growing up in twentieth-century America and have affected the way we dress, what jobs we pursue, the way we view history and the social issues we take seriously. In the most immediate sense, the cinema, after a century in existence, is still the most vital meeting ground in our society, allowing the entire community more now than ever to meet, share the experience of a movie and know that regardless of their incomes, color of skin or religion, they all share a strong bond as members of what has become an international community, the community of cinema.

Bibliography

Adorno, Theodor W., and Max Horkheimer. (1972). *The Dialectic of Enlightenment*. Trans. John Cumming. New York: Herder and Herder.

American Federation of Arts. (1987). *Before Hollywood—Turn-of-the-Century American Film*. New York: Hudson Hills Press.

Andres, Glenn M. (1993). "Urbanization and Architecture." In *Modern American Culture*, ed. Mick Gidley. New York: Longman.

Andrews, Wayne. (1978). *Architecture, Ambition and Americans A Social History of American Architecture*. New York: Free Press.

Arendt, Hanna. (1979). *The Recovery of the Public World*. Ed. Melvin Hill. New York: St. Martin's Press.

Atlanta Fox Web site. (2002). www.foxtheatre.org/history.htm. February.

Banerjee, Tridib. (1990). "Third World City Design: Values, Models and Education." In *Breaking the Boundaries*, ed. Bishwapriya Sanyal. New York: Plenum Press.

Barnouw, Erik. (1974). *Documentary: A History of the Non-Fiction Film*. Oxford: Oxford University Press.

Beardsley, Charles. (1983). *Hollywood's Master Showman: The Legendary Sid Grauman*. New York: Cornwall Books.

Bell, Daniel. (1973). *The Coming of Post-Industrial Society: A Venture in Social Forecasting*. New York: Basic Books.

Bergman, Andrew. (1972). *We're in the Money: Depression America and Its Films* New York: Harper and Row.

Black, Mary. (1973). *Old New York in Early Photographs: 1853–1901*. New York: Dover.

"Boeckh's Manual of Appraisal, 1934." (1998). *Marquee* 30(3).

Boyer, Christine. (1985). *Manhattan Manners: Architecture and Style: 1850–1900*. New York: Rizzoli.

Bradbury, Katherine, Anthony Downs, and Kenneth A. Small. (1982). *Urban Decline and the Future of American Cities*. Washington, DC: Brookings Institution.

Bush, W. Stephen. (1912). "Queen Elizabeth." *Moving Picture World*, October.

Bushnell, Horace. (1864). "City Plans." In *Work and Play; or Literary Varieties*. New York: Charles Scribner.

Castells, Manuel. (1996). *The Rise of the Network Society*. Oxford: Blackwell.

Castells, Manuel, and Peter Hall. (1994). *Technopoles of the World: The Making of 21st Century Industrial Complexes*. London: Routledge.

Charney, Leo and Vanessa R. Schwartz, eds. (1995). *Cinema and the Invention of Modern Life*. Berkeley: University of California Press.

Clarke, David B., ed. (1997). *The Cinematic City*. New York: Routledge.

"The Closing of Nickelodeons in New York City." (1907). *Moving Picture World* 1, 16 March.

Cotkin, George. (1992). *Reluctant Modernism: American Thought and Culture, 1880–1900*. New York: Twayne.

Davies, Philip and Brian Neve, eds. (1981). *Cinema, Politics and Society in America*. Manchester: Manchester University Press.

Davis, Michael. (1992). "Fortress LA: The Militarization of Urban Space." In *Variations on a Theme Park*, ed. Michael Sorkin. New York: Hill and Wang.

Davis, Mike. (1993). "Who Killed Los Angeles? A Political Autopsy." *New Left Review* 197(1): 3–28.

Debord, Guy. (1983). *Society of the Spectacle*. Detroit: Black and Red.

DeNevi, Donald P. and Doris A. Holmes, eds. (1973). *Racism at the Turn of the Century: Documentary Perspectives 1870 through 1910*. San Rafael: Leswing Press.

"Digital Juggeranut." (1994). *Business Week*, 13 June, 36–39.

Dizard, Wilson P. (1986). *The Coming Information Age: An Overview of Technology, Economics and Politics*. New York: Longman

Du Bois, W.E.B. (1933). "On Being Ashamed of Oneself." *Crisis Magazine*, September.

Dunlap, David W. (1990). *On Broadway: A Journey Uptown over Time*. New York: Rizzoli.

Dupuy, Gabriel. (1992). "New Information Technology and Utility Management." In *Cities and New Technologies*, pp. 51–76. Paris: OECD.

Dutton, William, ed., with the assistance of Malcolm Peltu. (1996). *Information and Communication Technologies: Visions and Realities*. Oxford: Oxford University Press.

Dutton, William, Jay Blumler, and Kenneth L. Kraemer, eds. (1987). *Wired Cities: Shaping the Future of Communicaton.* Washington Program, Annenberg School of Communications. Boston, Mass.: G.K. Hall.

Dyckman, Jack, Tridib Banerjee, and Alan Kreditor. (1984). "Planning in an Unprepared Environment." *The Planning Report* 55(2).

Eaton, Walter. (1908). *The American Stage of Today.* Boston: Small, Maynard and Company.

"Ed. White's Church Film Parties." (1912). *Moving Picture World,* 19 June.

Edge, David, and Robert Williams. (1996). *The Social Shaping of Technology.* Vol. 25. Edinburgh: Research Center for Social Sciences.

Edwards, Paul K. (1969). *The Southern Urban Negro as Consumer.* College Park: McGrath Publishing Company.

Encyclopedia of Exhibition. (1998). North Hollywood, CA: National Association of Theatre Owners.

Fielding, Ray. (1972). *The American Newsreel.* Norman: University of Oklahoma Press.

Film Daily Yearbook. (1929). New York: Variety.

Fiske, John. (1994). *Media Matters: Everyday Culture and Political Change.* Minneapolis: University of Minnesota Press.

Fitzgerald, Thomas. (1991). "Media, Ethnicity and Identity." *Media Culture, & Society.* 13: 193–214.

Ford, Larry. (1994). *Cities and Buildings: Skyscrapers, Skid Rows and Suburbs.* Baltimore: Johns Hopkins University Press.

Forsher, James and Tridib Banerjee, producers. (1995). *Invented Streets.* Unpublished Video Presentation.

Foucault, Michel. (1979). *Discipline and Punishment, the Birth of the Prison.* New York: Vintage Books.

Freidberg, Anne. (1993). *Window Shopping: Cinema and the Postmodern.* Berkeley: University of California Press.

Friedman, George. (1981). *The Political Philosophy of the Frankfurt School.* Ithaca and London: Cornell University Press.

Fuld, Horace. (1914). "Exhibiting the Picture." *The New York Dramatic Mirror,* 14 January, 54.

Gans, Herbert. (1991). *People, Plans and Policies.* New York: Columbia University Press and Russell Sage Foundation.

Garraty, John A. (1986). *The Great Depression* New York: Harcourt Brace Jovanovich.

Goddard, John and Ranald Richardson. (1996). "Why Geography Will Still Matter: What Jobs Go Where?" In *Information and Communication Technologies: Visions and Realities,* ed. William Dutton with assistance by Malcolm Peltu, pp. 196–214. Oxford: Oxford University Press.

Gottman, Jean. (1983). *The Coming of the Transactional City.* College Park: University of Maryland, Institute for Urban Studies.

Graham, Stephen and Simon Marvin. (1996). *Telecommunications and the City: Electronic Spaces, Urban Places.* London: Routledge.

Griffith, D.W. (1915). Editorial Response. *New York Globe,* 10 April.

Habermas, Jurgen. (1974). Article in the *New German Critique.*

Hulfish, David S. (1918). *Cyclopedia of Motion Picture Work.* Chicago: American Technical Society.

Hall, Ben M. (1961). *The Best Remaining Seats.* New York: Clarkson Potter.

Harrison, Louis Reeves. (1912). "The Exhibitor's Opportunity." *Moving Picture World,* 11 August.

Harvey, David. (1985). *The Urbanization of Capital.* Oxford: Blackwell.

Harvey, David. (1989). *The Conditions of Postmodernity.* London: Basil Blackwell.

Haws, Robert, ed. (1978). *The Age of Segregation: Race Relations in the South, 1890–1945.* Jackson: University Press of Mississippi.

Hepworth, M. (1986). "The Geography of Technological Change in the Information Economy." *Regional Studies* 20(5): 407–424.

Hepworth, Mark and Kenn Ducatel. (1992). *Transport in the Information Age: Wheels and Wires.* London: Belhaven Press.

Hinsley, Curtis M., Jr. (1981). *Savages and Scientists: The Smithsonian Institution and the Development of American Anthropology, 1846–1910.* Washington, D.C.: Smithsonian Institution Press, 1981.

Irwin, Will. (1928). *The House That Shadows Built.* New York: Doubleday.

Jacobs, J. (1962). *The Death and Life of Great American Cities.* New York: Random House.

Jameson, F. (1984). "Postmodernism, or the Cultural Logic of Late Capitalism." *New Left Review* 146: 53–92.

Jarvie, I.C. (1977). *Movies and Society.* New York: Basic Books.

Johnston, Eric. (1950). "Messengers from a Free Country." *Saturday Review of Literature,* 4 March.

Laterrassee, J. (1992). "The Intelligent City: Utopia or Tomorrow's Reality?" In *Telecom, Companies, Territories,* ed. F. Rowe and P. Veltz. Paris: Presses De L'ENPC.

Lee, Alfred McClung and Elizabeth Briant Lee. (1939). *The Fine Art of Propaganda.* New York: Harcourt Brace & Company.

Levi-Strauss, Claude. (1983). *The View from Afar.* Chicago: University of Chicago Press 1–40.

Lewis, George H. (1981). "Taste Cultures and Their Composition: Towards a New Theoretical Perspective." In *Mass Media and Social Change,* ed. Elihu Katz and Tamás Szecsko. Beverly Hills, Calif.: Sage Publications.

Lewis, Howard T. (1933). *The Motion Picture Industry.* New York: D. Van Nostrand.

Lightner, E.W. (1919). "Downtown Nickelodeon." *The Dispach,* 16 November. (Carnegie Library of Pittsburgh Web site: http://www.clpgh.org/exhibit/neighborhoods/downtown/down_n71.html.)

Lo Magazine. (1944). 1 October, 3.

Long, Norton. (1972). *The Unwalled City: Reconstituting the Urban Community.* New York: Basic Books.

Longstreth, Richard. (1998). *City Center to Regional Mall.* Cambridge, Mass.: MIT Press.

Loukaitou-Sideris, Anastasia and Tridib Banerjee. (1996). *Urban Design Downtown: Poetics and Politics of Form.* Berkeley: University of California Press.

Lynch, Kevin. (1981). *Good City Form.* Cambridge, Mass.: MIT Press.

Lynd, Robert S. and Helen Merrell Lynd. (1929). *Middletown.* New York: Harcourt, Brace and Company.

Lynd, Robert S. and Helen Merrell Lynd. (1937). *Middletown in Transition.* New York: Harcourt, Brace and Company.

Mackenzie, Donald and Judy Wajcman, eds. (1985). *The Social Shaping of Technology.* Philadelphia: Open University Press.

Mandlebaum, Seymour. (1986). "Cities and Communication: The Limits of Community." *Telecommunication Policy,* June: 132–140.

Mansell, Robin. (1996). "The Bias of Information Infrastructures." In *Information and Communication Technologies: Visions and Realities,* ed. William Dutton, with the assistance of Malcolm Peltu, pp. 438–470. Oxford: Oxford University Press.

May, Larry. (2000). *The Big Tomorrow.* Chicago: University of Chicago Press.

McKeon, Elizabeth and Linda Everett. (1998). *Cinema under the Stars: America's Love Affair with the Drive-in Movie Theater.* Nashville: Cumberland House.

Miles, Ian. (1999). "ICT Innovations in Services." In *Society on the Line: Information Politics in the Digital Age,* ed. William Dutton, with the assistance of Malcolm Peltu, pp. 96–107. Oxford: Oxford University Press.

Mitchell, W. (1995). *City of Bits: Space, Place and the Infobahn.* Cambridge, Mass.: MIT Press.

Modern Cinemas. (1936). London: Architectural Press

Morgan, Kevin. (1992). *Digital Highways: The New Telecommunications Era.* Cardiff: Department of City and Regional Planning, University of Wales College of Cardiff.

Morgan, Lewis Henry. (1877). *Ancient Society.* New York: Henry Holt & Co.

Motion Picture Herald. (1934). 11 August.

Moving Picture World. (1907). 16 March, 1(2).

Moving Picture World. (1907). 11 May.

Mumford, Lewis. (1924). *Sticks and Stones.* New York: Dover.

Mumford, Lewis. (1938). *The Culture of the Cities.* New York: Harcourt, Brace and Company.

Mumford, Lewis. (1966). *Technics and Human Development: The Myth of the Machine Volume One.* New York: Harcourt, Brace and Jovanovich.

Muvico public relations announcement. (1999). Ft. Lauderdale, FL.

Nasaw, David. (1993). *Going Out: The Rise and Fall of Public Amusements*. New York: Basic Books.

Naylor, David. (1981). *American Picture Palaces*. New York: Van Nostrand Reinhold Company.

"The Nickelodeon." (1907). *Moving Picture World*, 4 May, 1(9).

Nye, David E. (1990). *Electrifying America: Social Meanings of a New Technology*. Cambridge: MIT Press.

Openshaw, S. and J. Goddard. (1987). "Some Implications of the Commodification of Information and the Emerging Information Economy for Applied Geographical Analysis in the UK." *Environment and Planning A* 19: 1423–1439.

"Opinion of a Wise Old Judge." (1912). *Moving Picture World*, 20 July.

Parish, James Robert, and Michael R. Pitts. (1976). *The Great Gangster Pictures*. Metuchen NJ: Scarecrow Press.

Parson, Talcott. (1973). "Culture and Social Systems Revisited." In *The Idea of Culture in the Social Sciences,* ed. Louis Schneider and Charles M. Bonjean. Cambridge: Cambridge University Press.

Paschal, Andrew G. (1971). *A W.E.B. Du Bois Reader*. New York: The Macmillan Company.

"The Picture and the Church." (1912). *Moving Picture World*, 20 July.

Pildas, Lucinda. (1980). *Movie Palaces*. New York: Clarkson N. Potter.

Pool, I. de Sola. (1990). *Technologies without Boundaries*. Cambridge, Mass.: Harvard University Press.

Pool, I. de Sola, ed. (1977). *The Social Impact of the Telephone*. Cambridge, Mass.: MIT Press.

Putnam, Robert E. (1995). "Bowling Alone: America's Declining Capital." *Journal of Democracy* 6(1): 65–77.

Ramsaye, Terry. (1926). *A Million and One Nights: A Modern Classic*. New York: Simon & Schuster.

Ricketson, Frank H. (1938). *The Management of Motion Picture Theatres*. New York: Modern Technical Book Co.

Rifkind, Carole. (1977). *Main Street: The Face of Urban America*. New York: Harper.

Rogin, Michael. (1994). "The Sword became a Flashing Vison." In *The Birth of a Nation: D.W. Griffith, Director*, ed. Robert Lang. New Brunswick, N.J.: Rutgers University Press.

Rothstein, Edward. (1998). "A Shifting American Landscape." *New York Times,* 6 December.

Rousseau, Jean-Jacques. (1968). *The Social Contract*. Harmondsworth, Eng.: Penguin.

Sanyal, Bishwapriya, ed. (1990). *Breaking the Boundaries*. New York: Plenum Press.

Savitch, H. (1988). *Post Industrial Cities: Politics and Planning in New York, Paris, and London*. Princeton: Princeton University Press.

Schaffer, Daniel. (1982). *Garden Cities for America*. Philadelphia: Temple University Press.

Schneider, David. (1968). *American Kinship: A Cultural Account*. Englewood Cliffs: Prentice Hall.

Schultz, Stanley K. (1989). *Constructing Urban Culture*. Philadelphia: Temple University Press.

Segrave, Kerry. (1992). *Drive In Theaters: A History from Their Inception in 1933*. Jefferson N.C.: McFarland Press.

Sennett, Richard. (1977). *The Fall of Public Man*. New York: Knopf.

Sennett, Richard. (1990). *The Conscience of the Eye*. New York: Knopf.

Shand, P. Morton. (1930). *Modern Picture-Houses and Theaters*. Philadelphia: J.B. Lippincott.

Silva, Fred. (1971). *Focus on The Birth of a Nation*. Englewood Cliffs: Prentice Hall.

Soja, Edward. (1992). "Inside Exopolis: Scenes from Orange County." In *Variations on a Theme Park: The New American City and the End of Public Space*, ed Michael Sorkin. New York: Hill and Wang.

Sorkin, Michael, ed. (1992). *Variations on a Theme Park: The New American City and the End of Public Space*. New York: Hill and Wang.

Squires, J. (1994). "Private Lives, Secluded Spaces: Privacy as Political Possibility" *Environment and Planning D: Society and Space* 12: 387–401.

Stones, Barbara. (1993). *America Goes to the Movies: One Hundred Years of Motion Picture Exhibition*. North Hollywood: National Association of Theatre Owners.

Sullivan, Louis. (1990). *Louis H. Sullivan: A System of Architectural Ornament*, ed. Lauren Weingarden. New York: Rizzoli, in cooperation with the Art Institute of Chicago.

Tharp, Margaret Farrand. (1939). *America at the Movies*. New Haven: Yale University Press.

Theatre Catalogue. (1947). Philadelphia: Emanuel Publications, Inc.

Tocqueville, Alexis de. (1971). *Journey to America*. Translated by George Lawrence. Edited by J.P. Mayer. Garden City, NY: Doubleday.

Valentine, Maggie. (1994). *The Show Starts on the Sidewalk*. New Haven: Yale University Press.

Vance, James (1971). "Focus on Downtown." In *Internal Structure of the Cities: Reading Space and Environment*, ed. Larry Bourne. New York: Oxford University Press, 112–120.

Vasey, Ruth. (1993). "The Media." In *Modern American Culture*, ed. Mick Gidley. New York: Longman Publishing.

Vellela, Tony. (2001). "They Refused to Allow Their Town to Die." *Parade Magazine*, 12 August.

Webber, Melvin. (1963). "Order in Diversity: Community Without Propinquity." In *Cities and Space: The Future Use of Urban Land,* ed. Lowdon Wingo, Jr. Baltimore: Johns Hopkins University Press.

Webber, Melvin. (1964). "The Urban Place and the Non Place Urban Realm." In *Explorations into Urban Structure,* ed. M. Webber, J. Dyckman, D. Foley, A. Guttenberg, W. Wheaton and C. Whurster. Philadelphia: University of Pennsylvania Press.

Webber, Melvin. (1968). 'The Post-City Age." *Daedalus,* fall.

Weinberg, Meyer, ed. (1970). *W.E.B. Du Bois: A Reader.* New York: Harper and Row.

Weintraub, Jeff. (1995). *Varieties and Vicissitudes of Public Space in Metropolis: Center and Symbol of Our Times.* New York: New York University Press.

West, Nathanael. (1933). *Day of the Locust.* New York: New Directions Books

Winner, Langdon. (1992). "Silicon Valley Mystery House." In *Variations on a Theme Park,* ed. Michael Sorkin. New York: Hill and Wang.

Wirth, Louis (1938). "Urbanism as a Way of Life." *American Journal of Sociology* 44(1).

Wolfe, Tom (1981). *From Bauhaus to Our House.* New York: Farrar Straus Giroux.

Zuboff, Shoshana. (1984). *In the Age of Smart Machines.* New York: Basic Books.

Zukor, Adolph. (1953). *The Public Is Never Wrong.* New York: Putnam.

Index

Page references in *italics* indicate photographs of theaters.

About the Author

JAMES FORSHER is the Director of the Media Production Program
at California State University, Hayward.